"In this highly readable primer, Jonatha[n]  the nature of the Lord's Supper and show[s] Christian life and worship by drawing on [a range] of primary sources."

Dr. Simon Chan, Association of Theological Education
of Southeast Asia

"From the opening lines to the closing statements of *The Lord's Supper*, Jonathan had my undivided attention. As a Pentecostal, I was deeply stirred by the way he unfolded the significant passages in Scripture from Sinai to the Marriage Supper of the Lamb regarding the profound mystery of the sacramental grace that is ours in the Lord's Supper. Jonathan adeptly grasps the mysteries that enable us to "taste and see," through Eucharistic bread and wine, that the Lord is good. There is much here to feast upon for leadership and laity, scholar and student, disciple and devotee. As we move forward in this day of unprecedented change and unparalleled opportunity for Gospel mission, may we realize that the sustaining food for this pilgrim journey is ever found in the sacred Bread and Beverage that is Christ's Body and Blood."

Bishop Mark J. Chironna, Church On The Living Edge

"In this wonderful, deeply devotional book, pastor and theology lecturer Jonathan Black brings a timely, tender and passionate call for us to encounter Jesus afresh in the Lord's Supper. As we share in the Lord's Supper we are drawn to fresh wonder and worship and awakened to greater expectancy and faith."

Chris Cartwright, general superintendent
of Elim Pentecostal Churches

"The risen Jesus, wonderfully, is present to us exactly as we need Him to be (if not always the way we want). And what we need more than anything is for Jesus to be present to us *sacramentally*—as and in the mystical communion of the visible and the invisible, the earthy and the heavenly, the human and the divine in the feast of His body and blood. Tragically, many of our churches have lost touch with this mystery and its life-giving power. But, as Jonathan Black shows so convincingly in this timely, wise and badly needed book, the teaching of the Scriptures and the wisdom of the broader Christian tradition is clear: There, at Christ's table, thanks to the Spirit, we receive all the good the Father wants for us and intends for us to share with the world."

Chris Green, professor of Public Theology at Southeastern University

"Reading, I imagined myself in a living room with other Christians listening to Jonathan speak. His style is enthusiastic: part testimony, part biblical study and part historical survey, building a case for Christians to come to the Lord's Supper expecting nothing less than to meet the Lord."

The Right Reverend Gregory O. Brewer, Episcopal
Diocese of Central Florida

"I've had the great privilege of knowing Jonathan Black for many years as a friend, a gifted teacher of God's Word and a powerful authentic prophetic voice.

There are very precious moments in Church history when the light of revelation brings illumination that shifts the posture of the Church, which has the effect of realigning the Body of Christ with Christ, the Head of the Church, and advancing it on its mission on earth. We see these throughout history, some even in our lifetime. I sense that Jonathan's book and its brilliant and inspiring content will play a vital part in bringing about another needed shift. *The Lord's Supper* is carefully crafted in such a way that it inspires the reader to desire the privilege of Communion, and to seek deeper encounters and transformation in a fresh, meaningful and irresistible way. This personal inspiration is further intensified by the renewed understanding that Jonathan shares, and it refreshes the heart to know that as we engage afresh in Communion expectantly, we do so with all the saints, past and present, with all of heaven and most wonderfully with Christ Himself. Who wouldn't want to experience that again and again?

I thoroughly recommend you read it."

Ivan Parker, national leader, The Apostolic Church UK

"This book by Jonathan Black on the Lord's Supper is both thoroughly biblical, pastoral and devotional. If found it a very encouraging book to read, with helpful and deep insights that people from a variety of denominational backgrounds will find strengthening and encouraging."

The Right Reverend David A. McClay,
Bishop of Down and Dromore

The
LORD'S
SUPPER

The
LORD'S
SUPPER

*Our Promised Place of Intimacy and
Transformation with Jesus*

Jonathan Black

Chosen

a division of Baker Publishing Group
Minneapolis, Minnesota

© 2023 by Jonathan Black

Published by Chosen Books
Minneapolis, Minnesota
www.chosenbooks.com

Chosen Books is a division of
Baker Publishing Group, Grand Rapids, Michigan

Printed in the United States of America

Library of Congress Cataloging-in-Publication Data
Names: Black, Jonathan, 1982- author.
Title: The Lord's Supper: our promised place of intimacy and transformation with Jesus / Jonathan Black.
Description: Minneapolis, Minnesota: Chosen Books, a division of Baker Publishing Group, [2023] | Includes bibliographical references.
Identifiers: LCCN 2022058976 | ISBN 9780800763213 (trade paper) | ISBN 9781493441037 (ebook)
Subjects: LCSH: Lord's Supper--Pentecostal churches.
Classification: LCC BX8762.Z5 B525 2023 | DDC 234/.163—dc23/
eng/20230214
LC record available at https://lccn.loc.gov/2022058976

Cover design by Darren Welch Design

Baker Publishing Group publications use paper produced from sustainable forestry practices and post-consumer waste whenever possible.

23 24 25 26 27 28 29   7 6 5 4 3 2 1

To Jenny, Aaron, Barney & Josh,
who joined me nearly every day
in the Lord's presence at His table
in the good old days of the
daily breaking of bread.

CONTENTS

FOREWORD

WHEN YOU THINK of Pentecostal-charismatic meetings, you generally don't think of liturgy and sacraments. Instead, you think of free-form, contemporary worship, the gifts of the Spirit in operation, something spontaneous and, on a certain level, unrehearsed. As for liturgy and holy sacraments, that's for the more traditional churches, the older, denominational churches.

The problem for Pentecostals and charismatics is that the Bible is filled with liturgy, right into the New Testament, meaning that liturgy itself is not necessarily bad or anti-Spirit. As for sacraments, at a minimum, we Pentecostals and charismatics believe in the sacraments of baptism, communion, and the anointing of oil when praying for the sick. But have we thought about their meaning and significance? Do we truly understand their importance? And how can these practices be more deeply incorporated into our meetings, joining together sacrament and Spirit and Word?

We now have a book written by a young Pentecostal theologian whom I only know through the pages that follow and through the glowing recommendation of the publisher. Now you can get to know Jonathan Black for yourself as you read his new book. Better still, you can gain a better understanding of the sacrament of communion for yourself.

What really happens when we partake in communion together? What were the communion practices of the early church and how do those relate to us today? Where does communion fit in our public gatherings, home meetings, or personal time with the Lord? And what can we expect from Jesus when we share His bread and cup?

Within the Christian tradition, communion has different expressions and meanings. Some believe the bread and wine turn into the actual body and blood of Christ. Some deny the literal presence of Christ in the elements but say He is spiritually present, and others receive communion only as a symbolic act of remembrance. Regardless of your present stance, you will learn much as you read these pages, your thinking will be challenged on several points and, above all, you will receive a fresh invitation to partake of the Lord's transformational grace that is so freely poured out in and through His supper.

I, for one, want everything the Lord has given His Church. If it is from above. If it is good. If it is scriptural. If it glorifies Jesus. If it edifies—then I want it. And I don't want my own spiritual past to rob me in any way of God's best. Instead, I do my best to respond to Scripture, throwing out the bad and holding on to the good.

As you read Jonathan's book, especially when he contends that there is a strong connection between the Lord's Supper, the supernatural, transformation and revival, drink in his good insights, observations, and teachings. They might just impact your life in a lasting (even eternal) way.

Dr. Michael L. Brown, author, apologist,
and host of the *Line of Fire* radio broadcast

1

The Upper Rooms

D O YOU EVER FEEL like your eyes aren't fully open? I don't mean like me when I get out of bed in the morning, before I've made it as far as the kettle to make a cup of tea to properly wake up. I mean when you're fully awake but know there's much more to be seen than what your eyes can take in. And maybe, sometimes, we're even so used to our eyes not being fully open that we don't notice it. Everything looks normal, but we don't realize there is something far beyond what we are seeing.

A ROOM ON THE ROAD

On the very first Easter Day, two disciples had that experience. Their eyes weren't fully open, but they didn't realize it. The Lord Jesus was standing right beside them, walking with them and talking with them, but they didn't even recognize Him. All they saw was a fellow traveler on the road to Emmaus, when it was actually the Lord of glory who had just risen from the dead.

Now, to be fair, we can't blame the two disciples for not recognizing Jesus. It wasn't like we would have recognized Him any quicker. For Luke tells us, "Their eyes were restrained, so that they did not know Him" (Luke 24:16). Their eyes were restrained. Something was keeping them from seeing the reality. Jesus was really there. They could walk with Him and talk with Him. They could even have reached out and touched Him. He wasn't invisible or silent. He wasn't just there because He's God and so He's everywhere. He was there tangibly. They encountered Him, not just in a vision or a dream, but they saw Him and heard Him, and He made their hearts burn within them (see verse 32). They encountered Him in a glorious, powerful and tangible way—even if their eyes didn't yet recognize Him.

There came a point that evening when "Their eyes were opened and they knew Him" (verse 31), but it wasn't because they'd suddenly put the pieces together and figured out who He was. They didn't open their own eyes. They needed the Lord to open their eyes for them, and He did it in a rather unexpected way.

Jesus could have told them who He was as they walked along the road. After all, He did tell them a lot about Himself, for "Beginning at Moses and all the Prophets, He expounded to them in all the Scriptures the things concerning Himself" (verse 27). Jesus could have told them who He was when they invited Him in for supper. At that point, He could have told them He needed to get back to Jerusalem to appear to the disciples because *He* was the One who had just risen from the tomb. But He didn't.

Instead, "He went in to stay with them" (verse 29). They still didn't know who He was, but they were enjoying His company and displaying hospitality to a lone traveler. So they all sat down together at the table to eat. And when they did, "He took bread, blessed and broke it, and gave it to them" (verse 30). That's when their eyes were opened.

The Lord Jesus "was known to them in the breaking of bread" (verse 35). In fact, it was only once their eyes were opened to see Jesus in the breaking of bread that they realized the glorious reality of the encounter they'd been having the whole time. It was only when Jesus made Himself known to them in the breaking of bread that they said, "Did not our heart burn within us while He talked with us on the road, and while He opened the Scriptures to us?" (verse 32).

Jesus had been at work all along; He'd been doing something glorious. And the place where it all came together—the glory of the cross and the resurrection, the glory of the living Jesus and the glory of what He'd been doing in their lives as He opened His Word and made their hearts burn—was in the breaking of bread.

THE FIRST UPPER ROOM

In the room on the road, Jesus "took bread, blessed and broke it, and gave it to them" (verse 30). He'd done exactly the same thing only a few days before in a room down the road in Jerusalem.

On the night He was betrayed, "Jesus took bread, blessed and broke it, and gave it to them" (Mark 14:22). The supper

Jesus shared with the two disciples in Emmaus is pointing us back to the supper He had shared with His disciples in the Upper Room. He opened their eyes with a repeat of taking, blessing, breaking and giving.

In the Upper Room during the Last Supper, Jesus had promised to meet with His disciples in bread and wine by saying, "This is My body," and "This is My blood" (Matthew 26:26–27; Mark 14:22, 24).

Then Jesus was arrested, put to death on the cross and buried in the tomb. When we meet the two disciples on the road to Emmaus, they've already heard about an empty tomb and angels and the message that Jesus was alive, but they hadn't seen Him, and they don't know of anyone else who had either. But then Jesus took bread, blessed it, broke it and gave it to them. This wasn't just any old gesture. These actions restated the promise He had made only a few days earlier. To show them He was fulfilling that promise, He opened their eyes and revealed Himself to them in the breaking of bread.

Now, maybe you're thinking, *Sure, that all sounds very nice, but where's the promise? At the Last Supper, Jesus just told us to remember Him.* The thing is, Matthew and Mark say nothing at all about remembrance. Yes, Jesus tells us to "Do this in remembrance of Me" in Luke (22:19) and 1 Corinthians (11:24–25), but Matthew and Mark do not include that bit. So that must mean that there's something else going on in the supper beyond this remembrance!

What we do read in the Bible *every* time Jesus instituted the Lord's Supper are His words "This is My body" (Matthew 26:26; Mark 14:22; Luke 22:19; 1 Corinthians 11:24). And each time He also says "this is My blood of the new covenant" (Matthew 26:28; Mark 14:24) or "the new covenant in My blood" (Luke 22:20; 1 Corinthians 11:25). (For now, let's not get too caught up in how precisely that could be His body and blood—we'll think some more about what that does or doesn't mean later on.) Jesus is about to go to the cross and lay down His life for the sins of the world, then rise again in glorious victory over death, hell, sin and the devil, before ascending to the Father's right hand. Yet, somehow, He still promises that He'll be with His disciples as they eat and drink at His table.

In presenting the disciples with His body and blood, Jesus is making them a tangible promise. He's not just leaving them with an idea to remember, but with the promise of His powerful presence. You can't get more present than body and blood.

Think about what we've learned from our Zoom fatigue during the lockdown of the pandemic. Video calls helped us stay in touch with the people we love. We could see them and hear them and feel some sort of connection with them. But it didn't take us long to discover that it wasn't the same as them being present with us in flesh and blood. I can still remember how amazing it felt the first time I was able to sit down for a meal with friends at their kitchen table after months of not being able to see real, live people! I'd seen them every week on Zoom, but seeing them in real life, in flesh and blood, was something far, far better.

That's the promise Jesus gives us. A promise of the real-life, flesh-and-blood kind of presence. The best kind. Now, maybe you're still a bit skeptical that this is what is going on here. So let me show you how we see the promise of His presence in another way in that Upper Room. But to do that we need to go to some mountains.

UP THE MOUNTAIN

The Lord's presence often comes with meals in the Bible. It is often with food that Jesus reveals His glory in the gospels. In fact, it's often with bread (John 6:1–14) and with wine (John 2:1–11). But the Lord makes His presence known at meals in the Old Testament too. When the Lord and two angels came to speak with Abraham at Mamre, they ate, and it was as they were eating that the Lord revealed Himself (Genesis 18:5–8).

A few hundred years later, when the Lord delivered the children of Israel from Egypt and brought them to Mount Sinai, we read about a very interesting meal (that we could very easily miss because it is surrounded by so many wonderful works of God). After the Lord had spoken His Ten Commandments to the people (Exodus 20:1–17), and after Moses "drew near the thick darkness where God was" to receive God's Law (Exodus 20:21), the Lord sent Moses back down to get "Aaron, Nadab and Abihu, and seventy of the elders of Israel" to bring them partway up the mountain to "worship from afar" (Exodus 24:1).

So, Moses heads down the mountain to fetch Aaron and the others, but before he brought them back up, he had one more task.

> Moses came and told the people all the words of the LORD and all the judgments. And all the people answered with one voice and said, "All the words which the LORD has said we will do." And Moses wrote all the words of the LORD. And he rose early in the morning, and built an altar at the foot of the mountain, and twelve pillars according to the twelve tribes of Israel. Then he sent young men of the children of Israel, who offered burnt offerings and sacrificed peace offerings of oxen

to the Lord. And Moses took half the blood and put it in basins, and half the blood he sprinkled on the altar. Then he took the Book of the Covenant and read in the hearing of the people. And they said, "All that the Lord has said we will do, and be obedient." And Moses took the blood, sprinkled it on the people, and said, "This is the blood of the covenant which the Lord has made with you according to all these words."

Exodus 24:3–8

What's going on? Why all this blood? Moses tells the people what the Lord has told him, and they promise that they will do what the Lord has spoken. Then sacrifices are offered to ratify this covenant. And as Moses sprinkles the blood over the people, he says, "This is the blood of the covenant"—the same words Jesus would say as He gave His disciples the cup of the new covenant in His blood in the Upper Room.

The proclamation that "This is the blood of the covenant" is immediately followed by Moses, Aaron, Nadab, Abihu and the seventy elders going up the mountain. And then, very abruptly, Exodus simply tells us they saw God.

And they saw the God of Israel. And there was under His feet as it were a paved work of sapphire stone, and it was like the very heavens in its clarity. But on the nobles of the children of Israel He did not lay His hand. So they saw God, and they ate and drank.

Exodus 24:10–11

They see the Lord. And even what they see merely under His feet is so glorious that it's like heaven itself. What they saw when they saw the Lord Himself is too glorious for even the Bible to describe! And what do they do in the presence of the Lord? They eat and drink. They see the most glorious sight they've ever laid eyes on. They see the God of Israel—the Lord Himself in glorious splendor. They see the indescribable majesty. And what do they do? They get out their picnic.

Only it's not a picnic. They are overwhelmed with the glorious sight of the God whose mere footstool is more spectacular than the finest sapphires of this earth. The Lord Himself has invited them up this mountain. The Lord Himself has invited them into His very presence. And He doesn't bring them in just to gaze from a distance. This isn't something that could have taken place equally well on Zoom. They're not invited just to look at a glorious sight. They are invited in to eat and drink in the presence of the Lord. That's intimate fellowship. It's a bit like after the lockdown, when we could finally sit down and eat with the people we love and enjoy their presence—only a billion times more glorious.

The funny thing is, the Lord calls this worshiping "from afar." The high and exalted One who reigns high over all, the One who is far beyond us, majestic in His holiness, draws near to those who have been sprinkled with the blood of the covenant. They "worship from afar" as they eat and drink in His presence. And He still does that today.

NEAR WHILE AFAR

This meal at the sapphire pavement on the side of the mountain seems like one of the most intimate encounters with the Lord in all of Scripture. And yet it is what the Lord calls worshiping from afar. If that is what afar looks like, what happens when someone gets even closer?

Moses leaves Aaron, Nadab and Abihu and the elders to continue to worship from afar when the Lord calls him up into His presence at the top of the mountain.

> Now the glory of the LORD rested on Mount Sinai, and the cloud covered it six days. And on the seventh day He called to Moses out of the midst of the cloud. The sight of the glory of the LORD was like a consuming fire on the top of the mountain in the eyes of the children of Israel. So Moses went into the midst of the cloud and went up into the mountain. And Moses was on the mountain forty days and forty nights.
>
> Exodus 24:16–18

Eating and drinking in the presence of the Lord from "afar" looked glorious. But drawing nearer than that looks terrifying. Gone are the sapphire pavements and the brilliance of heaven. Now instead we see dark clouds, silence and finally a consuming fire. What we see when Moses gets closer is an overwhelming presence far beyond what we can grasp. But a bit farther down the mountain, we saw a gloriously beautiful presence as the elders ate and drank in the presence of the Lord.

Somehow what's going on as they worship from afar by eating and drinking seems more inviting than what's going on at the top of the mountain. It's the same God and the same glory. But they see and experience it in completely different ways.

Notice one more thing: Moses doesn't actually describe what he saw or experienced. He only tells us what it looked like "in the eyes of the children of Israel" (Exodus 24:17). We don't know what the sight of the glory of the Lord looked like to Moses himself. We know that "Our God is a consuming fire" (Hebrews 12:29; Deuteronomy 9:3). So the terrifying glory the children of Israel saw was truly the glory of our God. Yet, somehow, in His grace, the Lord drew Moses into that consuming fire, not as a terrifying flame, but as a flame of love, so that the overwhelming glory Moses encountered was a transforming radiance that caused even his face to shine with the glory of God (see Exodus 34:29–30). Moses was drawn up by the Lord in His grace, after being sprinkled by the blood of the covenant and having eaten and drunk in the presence of the Lord. The only way to the glory at the top of the mountain was by the blood and the meal of the presence.

Now, Moses didn't go up to the top of the mountain alone. His "minister" goes up with him (Exodus 24:13 KJV). *Minister* is an odd word that is usually (but not always) used to describe the priests and Levites and those who minister to the Lord in the Tabernacle and the Temple. They were "ministers of the altar" (Joel 1:13 KJV). It can be just a word for a servant, but it is also linked specifically to service around God's altar and before the Ark of His presence (see 1 Chronicles 16:4). That's an interesting connection because we've just seen the young men offering sacrifices on the altar and Moses sprinkling the blood of the covenant on the altar before we came up the mountain.

But even more interesting is this minister who hovers in the background with barely a mention. He's called Joshua, but at this point in Israel's history there has been no mention of a Joshua. There is a young man called Hoshea, whose name Moses will eventually change to Joshua (see Numbers 13:16). But at this point there is no Joshua. So why does the Bible call Hoshea by the name Joshua in this mysterious mention on the side of the mountain? Well, the name *Joshua* means

"The Lord is salvation." His original name, *Hoshea*, meant "O save!" But Moses isn't climbing this mountain hoping that God will save him. He isn't approaching the consuming fire in fear that it will burn him up. Moses is being drawn up this mountain by the gracious God who has already delivered His people from their bondage in Egypt. He has brought them into covenant with Him so that He is their God and they are His people. Moses has been invited up by the saving God who has sprinkled him with the blood and fed him in His presence, the gracious Lord who is salvation.

Like Moses, we can never climb up into God's presence alone. We can only utterly depend on the Lord who is salvation. And Joshua reminds us of that. For his new name points us to something much greater than himself. He stays in the background here in Exodus 24 because ultimately Joshua is there not to draw attention to himself, but to lift our eyes to Someone Else whose name means "The Lord is salvation" (Matthew 1:21). Joshua is what we get when we translate his name from Old Testament Hebrew into English. But we're much more used to seeing that name translated from New Testament Greek into English—from Greek, the same name translates as *Jesus*.

Only Jesus can bring us into the presence of the Lord (see John 14:6; Hebrews 10:19–20). And He does that by sprinkling us with His blood—the blood of the new covenant—and sitting us down to eat and drink in His presence. When Jesus spoke those words in the Upper Room that night, He wasn't only pointing us *forward* to the cross, but He was also pointing us *back* to the promise of the glory and radiance of the presence of the Lord in Exodus 24. He was pointing us back to the sprinkled blood, the heavenly sapphire pavement and the consuming fire who is the Lord, our salvation. Those words, "This is My blood of the new covenant" are an invitation up the mountain to eat and drink in the presence of our glorious God.

Now, we might not experience the top of the mountain every time we come to the table. That's okay. In fact, it's more than okay—it's how things should be. Sometimes God gives us glimpses of the mountaintop like the children of Israel had, which overwhelm us with the holiness and the majesty of the consuming fire. Occasionally, the Lord in His abundant grace gives mountaintop experiences of the grandeur of His glory. But always, when we gather with His people at His table, we "have come to Mount Zion and to the city of the living God, the heavenly Jerusalem, to an innumerable company of angels, to the general assembly and church of the firstborn who are registered in heaven, to God the Judge of all, to the spirits of just men made perfect, to Jesus the Mediator of the new covenant, and to the blood of sprinkling that speaks better things than that of Abel" (Hebrews 12:22–24). The Lord Himself draws near from a distance through the meal as we "worship from afar," drawing us by the blood of the covenant into His radiant love. And like the elders of Israel, we eat and drink in the heavenly glory of the presence of the Lord. Although sometimes, like the two on the road to Emmaus, our eyes are restrained, and we don't quite realize the true glory of what is happening.

UP TO THE TEMPLE

When Moses went into the cloud at the top of the mountain, the Lord showed him the pattern of the Tabernacle. He started with the three things inside: the Ark of God's presence, the golden lampstand and the table for the showbread.

What is showbread? That might be its traditional name in English, but it will help us to understand it better by translating it another way—its Hebrew name simply means "Bread of the Presence." This bread was to be set on the golden table, next to "its flagons and bowls with which to pour drink offerings" (Exodus 25:29 ESV). So, bread and wine (for drink offerings) were to be set on this table before the Lord "always" (verse 30). That means that the Tabernacle and Temple not only had Bread of the Presence, but Bread and Wine of the Presence.

Just before receiving this revelation, Moses had eaten and drunk in the presence of the Lord on the sapphire pavement. Now the Lord tells him that His people need a constant memorial before Him of eating and drinking in His presence in the form of bread and wine. Then every Sabbath day, the priests were to eat this bread of God's presence (see Leviticus 24:8–9). This bread was only to be eaten in a holy place, because it was "most holy" (verse 9)—after all, it was the bread of the presence of the holy God.

But not only do we have holy bread and wine here connected to the promise of the presence of the Lord, but this bread is also a sign of God's everlasting covenant (verse 8). The covenant that was sealed in the blood sprinkled on the children of Israel at the foot of Mount Sinai, the covenant celebrated by eating and drinking in the presence of the Lord on the sapphire pavement, now has a perpetual sign and memorial (a remembrance, in fact) before the Lord in bread and wine.

So the bread and wine of remembrance—the bread and wine of the new covenant in Jesus' blood, given by Jesus in the Upper Room—don't only point us up Mount Sinai, but up to the Tabernacle and Temple on Mount Zion with their bread and wine of the presence as well—not just to the one-off events on the mountain, but to the perpetual sign that endured through the centuries—first in the Holy Place of the Tabernacle and then in the Temple. Right at the center of worship in the Temple every Sabbath day, fresh bread would be offered before the Lord by the priest. The bread and wine of the Lord's presence that had been on the table would be eaten and drunk. The table of the Bread of the Presence (with the bread and wine placed upon it) was one of the four most holy objects in the Temple (see Exodus 40:20–28). And this weekly offering and meal around the table was one of the most holy acts of worship.

Now, in the New Testament Church, Jesus has given us new bread and wine of His presence right at the heart of Christian worship, and we, as a royal priesthood (1 Peter 2:9), are all invited to eat and drink.

ANOTHER UPPER ROOM

A few years after Jesus made those promises of His presence in that Upper Room in Jerusalem, and after He opened the disciples' eyes to His presence in the breaking of bread in Emmaus, we read about another Upper Room where His powerful presence was known at the breaking of bread.

As Paul traveled around the eastern Mediterranean on his third missionary journey, he stopped for seven days in Troas. That means the church in Troas could have the great apostle, one of the most famous preachers in the world, preach on the Lord's Day. Can you imagine if your church was suddenly going to have the apostle Paul preach on Sunday? We'd probably be shouting about it from the rooftops (or, well, you know, whatever the social media equivalent might be). Everyone would want to make sure they were at church that day. But that's not quite what happens in Troas. The Bible tells us exactly why they came to church that Sunday, and it wasn't to hear Paul. Nope. The Christians in Troas had a much more important reason to crowd into their Upper Room, for "On the first day of the week . . . the disciples came together to break bread" (Acts 20:7). They didn't come for the celebrity preacher. They didn't gather for a challenging message. They came together for the same reason they gathered each and every Lord's Day: to break bread.

But this didn't turn out to be a normal Sunday service—something went disastrously wrong. As Paul was preaching a very long sermon (it was midnight and he was still preaching!) the unthinkable happened.

> There were many lamps in the upper room where they were gathered together. And in a window sat a certain young man named Eutychus, who was sinking into a deep sleep. He was overcome by sleep; and as Paul continued speaking, he fell down from the third story and was taken up dead.
>
> Acts 20:8–9

But that wasn't the end. For "Paul went down, fell on him, and embracing him said, 'Do not trouble yourselves, for his life is in him'" (verse 10). Eutychus was dead. But the Lord used Paul to raise him from the dead. What a church service! What would we do next if it happened in our church? Perhaps we'd spend time spontaneously celebrating and giving thanks and praise to God. Or perhaps the service would just end right then and we'd all rush out to tell everyone we could find about what had just happened. Either way, that would probably be the end of whatever had been planned for the rest of the service.

But what did the Christians of Troas do? In their joy and thankfulness, they went right back to the purpose of their gathering: the breaking of bread. Embracing Eutychus and being used by God to miraculously raise him from the dead wasn't the most important thing Paul did with his hands that night, for as soon as he told everyone that Eutychus was alive, Paul came back up to the Upper Room and broke bread (verse 11). The most spectacular miracle that probably nearly anyone in the Church had ever seen in their entire lives wasn't enough to overshadow partaking in the Lord's table, the true purpose of their coming together. No preaching (no matter how dynamic, or, in this case, no matter how long), no gifts of the Spirit (no matter how spectacular) could overshadow the Lord's promised presence in the breaking of bread. The Lord's table towers over testimony, praise and miracles in its centrality and importance. Yes, Eutychus had a powerful encounter with the Lord in being raised from the dead. But the whole assembly were promised a powerful encounter with the Lord in the breaking of bread.

So, in this book, I want to help us all be like the Christians in Troas—to come to the Lord's table with such expectancy and faith in Christ's promise of His presence, that nothing, not even the most glorious and spectacular miracles, could keep us away. And to know that, whether our eyes are restrained or opened, our hearts can burn within us as we encounter Jesus in His Supper.

2

The Holy One in Our Midst: Rekindling Awe and Dispelling Fear

BESIDE THE LORD'S TABLE in our college chapel, there is a stained-glass window. All the stained-glass windows in the chapel date from a time long before it belonged to a Pentecostal theological college, and so they represent a very different tradition in the life of the Church. When I first arrived, a large speaker partially hid the image on the window by the Communion table. But as we started to hold daily breaking of bread services, people started to spend a lot more time in that part of the chapel, and the unnoticed window behind the speaker was noticed.

"Who's Tarcisius?" asked a curious student who had been examining the window while I was putting away the chalice after the breaking of bread. I didn't know the answer. He's not exactly a towering figure of Church history. I went to have a look at the window. The stained glass showed a boy holding a palm branch (the sign of a martyr) and clutching something else in his hands. Then, in smaller pictures below it, there were two almost comic book–like panels: one showing Christians in prison, and the other showing the boy from the main image lying on the ground, facing toward the imprisoned Christians, while a crowd around him were pelting him with large stones. He still clasped something in his hands. Who was this Tarcisius? What was he doing? And what was he holding on to so tightly? I didn't know, but I wanted to. So I headed off to the library for some answers.

Tarcisius, it turns out, was a very early Christian martyr. He lived in Rome in the third century where he was part of the Church, possibly a deacon. During a time of fierce persecution (probably under the Emperor Valerian), Tarcisius was given the task of taking Communion to the members of the Church who had been imprisoned for their faith. (In those days, someone would be sent from the church service to take the elements to the sick and imprisoned from the same table around which the whole congregation was gathered for Communion so that the whole church was sharing in the same supper.) On the way from the Communion service to the prison, however, Tarcisius was attacked by a pagan mob who demanded that he hand over the sacrament. But Tarcisius refused. Instead, he clasped it more tightly to protect it with his life. Tarcisius was stoned to death when he wouldn't hand over the Communion. His martyrdom would go on to be lauded in poetry by a leader of the church in the city:

> Tarcisius was carrying the Sacrament of Christ
> When unclean hands sought to profane it.
> He preferred to lay down his life,
> Rather than betray the Holy Body to rabid dogs.[1]

Tarcisius became a martyr for the Lord's Supper. He gave up his life rather than give up the Communion bread, because Tarcisius knew the supper wasn't something to be taken lightly, as this wasn't just merely bread anymore.

Now, maybe that sounds mad to you. It's probably not the way we generally think about the bread and wine we receive in church at the Lord's Supper. But it didn't sound mad to Tarcisius at all. Nor to Damasus (the bishop who wrote the poem), nor to whoever designed the stained-glass window in the college chapel in a little village on top of a hill in the English countryside a millennium and a half later.

My students loved the story when I reported back on what I'd discovered. It was, after all, quite exciting and not at all what one might expect from a largely unnoticed window in a Pentecostal church. But I suspect they also thought it was a bit crazy. Such awe and reverence for the sacrament might be all very well for Catholics, but didn't the Reformation change all that?

Well, no. The Reformation didn't change that at all. The Lord's Supper was indeed a major issue in the Reformation, but both sides—Rome and the Reformers—held the supper in very high regard, because both sides—Catholic and

Protestant—believed Jesus was present in the supper. And so, both sides agreed that we should come to His table in awe and wonder to meet with the crucified and risen Savior.

THE REFORMATION RESTORATION OF THE BREAKING OF BREAD

Sometimes the stories that catch hold about the Reformation have somehow gotten separated from what really happened. Every year when I teach my doctrine class about the sacraments, someone will very confidently tell me that the Reformation got rid of the superstitious idea that Jesus was present in the sacrament. Somehow, we seem to have gotten the idea that the medieval church had transformed a simple meal into a complicated ritual to make Christ present, but then the Protestant Reformers came along and swept that all away, replacing the chalice of Christ's blood with some beakers of grape juice and getting us all back to the good old New Testament idea of remembering what Jesus has done. But none of that is true. Grape juice wasn't even invented until nearly four hundred years after the Reformation, and it isn't used for Communion by many Protestants around the world even today. The same is true with the little individual Communion cups (unheard of before the 1890s and still rejected by most Protestant churches around the world). None of that is anywhere near the heart of the Reformation's reforms of abuses around the Lord's Supper. There is always a danger in reading things into history and letting them take on an importance they never had, based on our own viewpoint. So let's go back into history and see what really mattered to the Reformers.

The Lord's Supper really was one of the most centrally debated issues of the Reformation, along with the supreme authority of Scripture and the doctrine of justification by grace alone, through faith alone. But the heart of the debates about the Lord's Supper might not be exactly what we've imagined. In fact, at the heart of the Reformers' concerns about the supper were the ways it connected with those other two big issues.

First, the supper should be celebrated according to Scripture. If Scripture is our supreme authority, then that's where we need to go to learn what to do when we gather to celebrate the sacrament. And if the Church, by way of its councils and bishops, is forbidding something Scripture teaches, then it is trying to usurp the authority of God in His Word. Which is exactly what the Reformers saw as happening in the late medieval church. The church in Western Europe had forbidden anyone who wasn't a priest from drinking from the cup. Instead, they received Communion "under one kind" (i.e., just the bread). But we read in Scripture that when the Lord Jesus instituted the Last Supper, He said, "Drink from it, all of you" (Matthew 26:27). So, the church, by forbidding the laity from receiving the cup, was going directly against the command of Christ. As Martin Luther put it, "if we permit one institution of Christ to be changed, we make all of his laws invalid, and any man may make bold to say that he is not bound by any other law or institution of Christ. . . . For here the word and example of Christ stand unshaken when he says, not by way of permission, but of command: 'Drink of it, all of you.'"[2] Therefore, "They are sinners, who forbid the giving of both kinds to those who wish [to receive]. The fault lies not with the laity, but with the priests . . . priests are not lords, but servants in duty bound to administer both kinds to those who desire them, as often as they desire them."[3]

And if Scripture is our supreme authority, how we explain what happens in the Lord's Supper can't contradict the words of Scripture. Scripture continues to use the word "bread" after it is consecrated and while it is eaten (see 1 Corinthians 10:16; 11:26–28). Yet, the late medieval (and now Roman Catholic) concept of transubstantiation insists that after the consecration, what is on the table is no longer bread and wine, but only the body and blood of Christ. (The accidents—the outward appearance, taste, texture, smell, etc.—of the bread and wine remain, but the substance of the bread and wine has been replaced by the substance of Christ's body and blood.) For the Reformers, this was contrary to the explicit words of Scripture, where it is still called "bread." Luther insisted that "it is an absurd and unheard-of juggling with words to understand 'bread' to mean 'the form or accidents of bread.'"[4] Rather, "no violence is to be done to the words of God, whether by man or angel . . . we have to think of real bread and real wine, just as we do of a real cup."[5] Now, this did not in any way mean that Luther (or the other Reformers, for that matter) denied Christ's presence in the supper. What they denied was the absence of bread and wine. (Luther believed "with a simple faith that Christ's body and blood are truly contained" in the supper, along with the bread and wine.[6])

The second concern the Reformers had regarding the supper was that it should not be a work we perform in order to earn God's grace. Luther saw this as "by far the most wicked of all" problems surrounding the sacrament, for "there is no opinion more generally held or more firmly believed in the church today than this, that the mass is a good work . . . so that the faith of the sacrament has become utterly extinct and the holy sacrament has been turned into mere merchandise, a market, and a profit-making business."[7] What he was getting at was that most people thought of the mass as a way of gaining God's favor. It wasn't receiving Communion (the eating and drinking) that was the most important thing, but having "the sacrifice of the mass" offered for you. Most people received Communion very rarely. But you could still go to church much more often to benefit from the sacrifice of the mass. You could even attend the service on behalf of someone else (or, by the time of the Reformation, pay a priest to offer a mass for you). In fact, many medieval churches have little windows called "squints" at just the right height and angle to let people look in and see the sacrifice of the mass being lifted up as the bell rang for the consecration, so they could benefit from it without even having to attend the service.

But the Reformers saw that this all ran counter to the Good News they were proclaiming of God's great grace to us in Christ alone. The way people were treating the sacrament was as if it was a human work we could perform to earn grace from God. Instead, Luther and the other Reformers wanted people to know that the sacrament is a place where we come to meet with Christ Himself, in whom alone grace is to be found. The supper is not our sacrifice offered to God, but God's gift offered to us.

And so, we are all invited to eat and drink, not just once in a while, but as often as we come to the Lord's table. The sacrament is not a spectator sport. A squint is of no use to us, because we haven't come to watch a priest offer a sacrifice on our behalf, but to "Taste and see that the LORD is good" (Psalm 34:8). The Lord's Supper isn't theater; it's a feast.

And to make that clear, the Good News of the Gospel had to be proclaimed out loud. The Reformers brought preaching back to the Communion service. They preached Christ boldly and faithfully before inviting the congregation to the table, so that everyone would know just who it was they were encountering in the supper and what glorious salvation He had accomplished for them. And then, at the table itself, they made sure that the most important words—Christ's own words—rang out loud and clear. In the medieval church, these words had been whispered by the priest in Latin. But now they are proclaimed out loud by the minister at the table so that everyone would hear Christ's proclamation of this Good News: "Take, eat; this is My body, which is given for you. This do in remembrance of Me.... Drink of it, all of you; this cup is the new testament in My blood, which is shed for you for the forgiveness of sins. This do, as often as you drink it, in remembrance of Me."[8]

The Reformation did address a lot of important problems with the way the Lord's Supper was being celebrated. But belief in Christ's presence wasn't one of these problems. The Protestant Reformers still drew near to the Lord's table in reverence and awe at the presence of the Lord.

THE REFORMATION REVERENCE FOR THE BREAKING OF BREAD

True reverence is revealed in actions. So let me give you two examples from the Reformation itself that demonstrate the great reverence in Christ's presence at His table, which has always been part of the Protestant approach to the supper.

Wittenberg is famous as the town where the Reformation began. It was there that Martin Luther nailed the *95 Theses* to the door of the castle church. And it was there that Luther continued to minister, as a faithful pastor to the flock. One day in 1542, he was, as usual, in church for the Communion service when something out of the ordinary (and yet also very ordinary) happened. A woman tripped as she knelt down to receive Communion and knocked the chalice so that it spilled. Both Martin Luther and Johannes Bugenhagen (another great leader of the Reformation, who was also a great theologian of the Lord's Supper) immediately ran over and knelt down on the floor to lick up the spilled wine. Eyewitnesses said that Luther's eyes were full of tears and he cried out, "O God, help!" For these two great Protestant Reformers, this was a catastrophe that had to be taken very seriously indeed. The contents of the chalice were far too precious to lie on a church floor.[9]

In Geneva, John Calvin famously demonstrated his reverence for the sacrament in a somewhat different way. On September 3, 1553, St. Peter's Cathedral was especially crowded. The people of the city knew that this was not going to be a run-of-the-mill Communion service. A group of wealthy and powerful citizens (the Libertines), who had been excommunicated for unrepentant immorality, entered the church, with their hands on the hilts of their swords, and sat down opposite the Communion table. They fully intended to take Communion by the power of the sword. Calvin, however, was undeterred by the blades. After blessing the bread and cup, he placed himself between the Libertines and the Lord's table, and declared: "These hands you may crush; these arms you may lop off; my life you may take; my blood is yours, you may shed it; but you shall never force me to give holy things to the profane, and dishonor the table of my God."[10] Like

Tarcisius, Calvin was ready to give his life to protect the sacrament; unlike Tarcisius, he didn't have to. The Libertines didn't dare approach the table. "The sacrament was celebrated with extraordinary silence, not without some degree of trembling, as if the Deity himself were actually present."[11] The whole city was struck by the power of Calvin's words and actions.

Neither Luther nor Calvin could take the Lord's Supper lightly. But it wasn't because either was overly concerned with ritual or formality. In fact, both these examples show them breaking the normal ritual and disrupting the niceties of the order of service because something much more important was at stake. For both Luther and Calvin, the supper demanded the utmost reverence and awe, because when we come to the supper, we come into the very presence of the Lord Himself.

PROTESTANTS AND PRESENCE

Protestants believe in the presence of Christ in the Lord's Supper. They haven't always agreed about exactly *how* Christ is present. But all the Protestant Reformers agreed *that* Christ is present. Even the great Baptist pastor Charles Spurgeon said, "We firmly believe in the real presence of Christ."[12] "He calls upon us to eat bread with Him; yea, to partake of Himself, by eating His flesh and drinking His blood."[13] If you're a bit hesitant about Spurgeon's words, let me just take you back to the Reformation briefly to see what the Protestant Reformers had to say about the presence of Christ in the supper.

For Martin Luther, Christ's presence in the supper was the very plain teaching of Scripture. Jesus said, "This is My body," so therefore this bread *is* His body. That means that the Lord's Supper is, as Luther put it in his *Small Catechism* (for parents to teach their children), "the true body and blood of our Lord Jesus Christ, under the bread and wine, for us Christians to eat and to drink, instituted by Christ Himself."[14] To say anything else was, as Luther saw it, to reject the plain meaning of Scripture, and so he declared that he'd rather drink pure blood with the Pope than "have mere wine with the fanatics."[15] In other words, while he argued that the Pope was wrong in denying the presence of bread and wine in the Lord's Supper, it was far less serious to deny the bread and wine than to deny Christ's body and blood (like the fanatics did).

One of those fanatics, Ulrich Zwingli,[16] lived down in Zurich. People today often think that Zwingli completely denied Christ's presence in the supper, but that wasn't the case at all. (The only people who actually denied Christ's presence in the supper altogether and said it was only something to remind us of what Christ had done were the Socinians, who did so because they also denied that Jesus is God.) Although Zwingli rejected Luther's teaching that communicants received the true body and blood of Christ along with the bread and wine, he did believe that Christians feed on Christ in the sacrament. For Zwingli, Christ's body "is not eaten literally and in its essence, but only spiritually, in the Lord's Supper."[17] Yet, he was adamant that he "never denied that the body of Christ is in the supper."[18] Christ's body is eaten and His blood is drunk, just in a different way. So Christ is present at His Supper, and Christ feeds His people with His body and blood at His Supper. But He does it (for Zwingli) while we are eating and drinking, as the bread and wine cause us to meditate in faith upon Christ and His sacrifice (rather than through the bread and wine themselves). Luther found this an intolerably low view of Christ's presence in the supper. Many Christians today might be shocked by how high a view of Christ's presence it is (especially compared to what people tend to say about Zwingli).

But, even among those churches where the Reformation was going ahead with reforms much more like Zwingli's than Luther's, many of the pastors and the people were rather uncomfortable with Zwingli's ideas about the Lord's Supper. They saw the serious divisions among the Reformation churches and didn't want to have to part company with Luther, as Zwingli had been forced to. Churches led by Martin Bucer and John Calvin saw that Zwingli had gone too far in his low view of Christ's presence in the supper. Christ's promise in Scripture was not just that His body and blood would be present to the hearts of believers, but that in eating this bread and wine, He would feed them with His body and blood. Calvin wrote: "When we speak of the communion which we have with Christ, we understand the faithful to communicate not less in His body and blood than in His Spirit, so that thus they possess the whole Christ. Now Scripture manifestly declares the body of Christ to be verily food for us and his blood verily drink. It thereby affirms that we ought to be truly nourished by them, if we seek life in Christ."[19] Calvin's view, and that of the churches that followed his lead, was much closer to Luther's understanding than that of Zwingli, although there were still significant differences. While for Luther, Christ feeds believers with His body and blood here on earth in the bread and wine of the supper, for Calvin, it was the Holy Spirit who lifted believers up into heaven through eating the bread and wine, to feed on Christ's body and blood there. Both Luther and Calvin believed that we meet with Christ in the supper and that He feeds us there with His body and blood. What they disagreed about was *how* exactly that happens.

And all the major Protestant confessions of faith flowing out of the Reformation take either Luther's view or Calvin's. (That includes the confessions of faith of the Lutheran, Reformed, Presbyterian, Anglican, Congregationalist, Particular Baptist, Wesleyan Methodist, Calvinistic Methodist churches and many others that have sprung from them.) And this isn't just an old idea that people used to have a few centuries ago. Even this decade (the 2020s), confessional statements have been produced by Anglicans, Wesleyans and Pentecostals proclaiming that "the Body and Blood of Christ . . . are truly taken and received in the Lord's Supper,"[20] that "His body and blood in this sacrament nourish our very bodies and souls,"[21] and that "in this sacrament the Lord by His Spirit takes up the products of human cultures (bread and wine), and blesses them by His Word (pronounced in the thousands of languages of this earth) so that through them He meets with us in His body and blood."[22]

So, three main approaches to the supper came out of the Reformation: Luther's, Zwingli's and Calvin's.[23] But all three agreed that Christ is indeed present. For centuries following, virtually all Protestants agreed on that. And, for the most part, we still do today.

PENTECOSTALS AND PRESENCE

A few weeks ago, I was preaching in a Pentecostal church in Belgium. After a time of praise and worship, the pastor stood up at the Communion table and said: "We have drawn near to Jesus in worship, but now we are drawing much closer to Him in the breaking of bread. The Lord's Supper is the best way to draw closest to Him."[24] This wasn't some new idea that a pastor in Belgium had come up with. Pentecostals have always believed this. As one prominent British Pentecostal leader of a previous generation put it, "Pentecostals love the communion service beyond all occasions [for] it is then . . . that the Lord draws the closest."[25] The breaking of bread is a foretaste of heaven on earth, for there "He whose presence makes heaven itself what it is, [is present] in our very midst."[26]

How can that be? Well, William Seymour, leader of the Azusa Street revival, had the answer to that question: At the Lord's Supper, "We eat His flesh and drink His blood."[27] Jesus is present in the supper in a way He isn't present anywhere else, because it is in the supper that He has promised to feed us with His body and blood. Yes, Protestants have always had some disagreements as to *how* that happens (and Pentecostals and charismatics continue that), but far more important than *how* He's present by His body and blood is the fact that He *is* present by His body and blood, just as He's promised. So, early Pentecostals could insist that, in the supper, "The Lord's presence is the main thing."[28]

And because they saw that the Lord's presence was the main thing in the breaking of bread, they took it very seriously indeed. Some early Pentecostals would spend "whole nights in prayer" before coming to receive the "Holy Sacrament with fear and trembling."[29] Yet, this fear was always "a healthy fear of God."[30] Being serious about the supper isn't a bad thing at all; it flows from reverence and awe for the Lord, whom we meet at His table.

AWE-FILLED WONDER

The "blessed" who "put their trust" in the Lord Jesus—those who "kiss the Son"—are called to worship Him "with fear, and rejoice with trembling" (Psalm 2:11–12). To come so close into the presence of our Savior that it can be described as a "kiss" is a fearful yet joyous occasion. Like the story of the woman with the alabaster jar, who washed the feet of Jesus with her tears and kissed Christ's feet in love (Luke 7:37–47), we draw near in love and thankfulness to the Savior who has washed us with His blood. That's what happens when we come to the Lord's table: As with our lips we partake of Christ's body and blood in bread and wine, we receive the kiss of the incarnate Son, the God who took on our flesh and gave Himself for us, and we "rejoice with trembling."

Like Moses at the burning bush, we stand on holy ground when we come to the Lord's table. Like the bush that burned, yet was not consumed, this bread and wine burns with the presence of the Savior, and yet bread and wine remain. And as our eyes are opened to see the burning reality of the presence of the Savior, our hearts burn within us, and we bow our hearts in reverence and awe.

That's why Calvin was willing to give his life for the supper. That's why Tarcisius did give his life for the supper. Maybe now that willingness seems a bit less mad.

3

Proclaiming the Cross

A T THE CENTER of the Christian faith stands the cross of Christ. In fact, the cross not only stands at the center of the Christian faith—it stands at the center of everything. Christ's cross is the center of history and the center of the universe. All of time and space finds its center at Golgotha. And the life of the Church, and the life of every Christian, flows from that life-giving tree where the Lamb of God was lifted up to die for the sins of the world.

And just as the life of the Church flows from the cross, so too the worship of the Church is centered on the cross. The very heart of the Church's worship is the table of the broken body and shed blood of Christ. As we meet around the Lord's table, we meet around the cross. And as often as we do, we "proclaim the Lord's death till He comes" (1 Corinthians 11:26).

SEEING THE GOOD NEWS

We proclaim the Lord's death as we explain what is happening at the table. As we hear the Gospel preached and then hear Christ's words, "This is My body which is broken for you" (1 Corinthians 11:24) and "This is My blood of the new covenant, which is shed for many for the remission of sins" (Matthew 26:28) spoken over the bread and wine, the Lord's death is proclaimed. But it is not only proclaimed in words; the Lord's death is proclaimed in the bread and wine themselves. "As often as you eat this bread and drink this cup, you proclaim the Lord's death" (1 Corinthians 11:26). The bread and wine themselves that we eat and drink proclaim the Good News of what Jesus has done for us through His death in our place on the cross. We don't only hear the Good News at the table; we see it and feel it and taste it as well.

So the supper is a sort of visible, tangible, gospel word. Most of us have probably heard Jesus' words over the bread and wine so many times, and know them so well, that just seeing the bread and wine on the Lord's table immediately starts to speak the Gospel of the cross to our hearts. As we see the pastor take up the bread in his hands and break it, we see the body of Christ torn by nail, and thorn, and spear. As we see him lift up the cup, we see the Lamb of God lifted up on the cross. As we see the wine shimmering in the chalice, we see the shed blood of the Savior, poured out for us to cleanse us of our sins. As we feel the bread on our tongues and the wine on our lips, we have that tangible proclamation that Christ not only died two thousand years ago on a hill outside Jerusalem, but He died for us—He died for you and for me. Each time I eat and drink at the Lord's table, the Good News of the cross—the Good News that Christ died for my sins and rose again for my salvation—is proclaimed to me afresh. I see it. I feel it. I taste it. And tasting, I know that the Lord is good, and He's good *for me*.

BROKEN FOR YOU, SHED FOR YOU

The Lord Jesus Himself proclaimed His own death at that first supper (which was the Last Supper) in the Upper Room on the night of His betrayal. "This is My body which is given for you. . . . This cup is the new covenant in My blood, which is shed for you" (Luke 22:19–20), He said. Although these words are so familiar to us that we're no longer surprised, the disciples in that Upper Room wouldn't have found them familiar at all. These were startling words the first time they were spoken (and still should be for us today, if we really think about them). Here Jesus proclaims the separation of His body and blood. His body is given and His blood is shed, and such separation of body and blood can only point to one thing: death. In the midst of the feasting, Jesus proclaims His death. But this is not only a prophetic announcement of His impending crucifixion. Christ does not simply tell the disciples that His body will be broken (see 1 Corinthians 11:24) and His blood shed—to that announcement of His death He adds a proclamation of the reason: "for you."

And that "for you" wasn't only for the twelve gathered with Jesus in the Upper Room. Jesus wasn't just saying "for you,

Peter; for you, James; for you, John" and "for you" to each of the rest of the Twelve around that table at the Last Supper. No! It extends beyond them to "many" (Matthew 26:28; Mark 14:24). He was saying "for you" to everyone who comes to Him in faith, to everyone who entrusts themselves to His broken body and His shed blood. He offers that promise to you today. Come to Him in faith and receive His body, broken for you, and His blood, shed for you, for the forgiveness of sins.

Maybe you're not so sure. You might be wondering, *How could what Jesus said to His twelve closest followers on the night before His death be meant for me today as well?* To answer that, let's jump forward a bit to another Upper Room scene. Fifty days after Jesus rose from the dead, the disciples gathered again in an upper room. But it wasn't just them. All in all, one hundred and twenty disciples were there, when, on that day—the Day of Pentecost—the Holy Spirit fell. And what was the result? Gospel preaching! Peter got up and preached to the crowd who had gathered to find out what was going on. And he told them of Jesus, and how He had died and rose again, and how He has been exalted to the right hand of the Father in heaven, from where He pours out the Holy Spirit on His people. And the crowd, when they heard this Good News, "were cut to the heart" (Acts 2:37), and asked Peter and the other apostles what they should do. "Repent, and let every one of you be baptized in the name of Jesus Christ for the remission of sins; and you shall receive the gift of the Holy Spirit," Peter told them (verse 38). Notice that Peter speaks to them about the remission of sins, which is exactly what Jesus had said about His blood at the Last Supper: "This is My blood of the new covenant, which is shed for many for the remission of sins" (Matthew 26:28).

Both Jesus and Peter were speaking the Good News about how people can be forgiven and set free from their sins. Jesus said this forgiveness was "for you," and Peter said the same thing to the crowd on the Day of Pentecost. He expanded on it a bit more to help us understand exactly whom Christ's promise of "you" is for: "For the promise is to you and to your children, and to all who are afar off, as many as the Lord our God will call" (Acts 2:39). Peter says that Jesus' promise of the remission of sins is for the people who are listening to him preach about Jesus, and for their children too, and their children's children—it's a promise for people of every generation and of every age. The promise of redemption through the shed blood of Jesus is a promise for men and women and boys and girls from "every tribe and tongue and people and nation" (Revelation 5:9). And that includes you. You don't need to worry if you're included in the "for you" that Jesus spoke in the Upper Room. Jesus has shed His blood for you, and He invites you to entrust yourself to Him and His shed blood on your behalf. "In Him we have redemption through His blood, the forgiveness of sins, according to the riches of His grace" (Ephesians 1:7).

Forgiveness and redemption are only found "in Him" and "through His blood," but they're for all who come to Him, trusting in His blood. Those words in the Upper Room are spoken to you today just as much as they were spoken to Peter, James and John then.

THE REMISSION OF SINS

Jesus gave His body and shed His blood "for you," which means there is a benefit for you in the broken body and shed blood of Jesus. He offered Himself up on the cross on your behalf, for your benefit. We'll look more at the benefits we receive from Christ in the supper in later chapters, but for now let's focus on the remission of sins—what Jesus proclaimed when He instituted the supper.

Remission isn't a word we tend to use much today. The context in which we most often hear it today is when a disease is referred to as *in remission*. The remission of sins is not like that. If a disease is in remission, it's still lurking and might return. When Jesus remits sin, it has been cancelled forever. The debt has been fully paid. The penalty has been completely removed. The remission of sins means full forgiveness. And this full forgiveness is right at the heart of what Jesus proclaims in the supper.

But Jesus doesn't only proclaim full forgiveness; He proclaims the *way* our sins are forgiven. Forgiveness comes only through the shed blood of Jesus. It is not something we can earn for ourselves. We can't try to impress God, hoping one day He'll let us off the hook for our sins—no! There is only one way for our sins to be forgiven, for "without shedding of blood there is no remission" (Hebrews 9:22). And that sin-remitting blood could only be the blood of Jesus (see Hebrews 10:4, 19–23).

But what does it mean for Jesus' blood to be shed? It's true, Jesus bled for us at Calvary. The cruel thorns of the mockers' crown tore into His head. His hands and feet were pierced by the executioner's nails. And then, at the end, the spear was thrust into His side "and immediately blood and water came out" (John 19:34). But that isn't what killed Him. He was already dead. Jesus did bleed on the cross, but He didn't die by bleeding. That is not how crucifixion killed.

The significance of Jesus' blood being shed wasn't so much in the manner of His death as the meaning of His death. For us today, bloodshed is a concept linked with violent death. But for those who heard Jesus' words of institution at the supper, the shedding of blood had a different connotation altogether. This wasn't the language of violence, but of sacrifice.

We might miss this, because often our English Bibles use "shed" in the New Testament for Jesus' words at the supper, but "poured" for the blood of the Old Testament sacrifices. Yet it's exactly the same idea. The word Jesus uses for "shed" in the Upper Room is the same word that's used in the Greek translation of the Old Testament (which the early Christians used) for the blood poured out in the sacrifices of the Tabernacle. So when Jesus says this is His blood that is shed for us, He's saying that it's poured out for us—and by that He means *poured out as a sacrifice*.

The type of sacrifice the pouring out of blood particularly points to is the sin offering, in which the blood of the sacrifice was poured out at the base of the altar (see Leviticus 4:7–8, 18, 25, 30, 34; 8:15; 9:9). The sin offering was a sacrifice offered for forgiveness (see Leviticus 4:24–26). So by speaking of shed blood for the remission of sins, Jesus wants us to understand that He is our true sin offering. He has offered Himself up on the cross as our sin offering to bring us forgiveness.

But if Jesus fulfills the sin offering for us, He must fulfill the whole of the sin offering. The shedding of blood at the base of the altar wasn't the entirety of this sacrifice. Before the blood was poured out, it was sprinkled (either in the Holy Place, in front of the veil and on the horns of the altar of incense, or on the horns of the altar of burnt offering, depending upon whose sin was being forgiven—the priest and congregation of Israel or an individual) and then (in the case of a sin offering for an individual) the meat of the offering was eaten as holy food by the priest in the court of the Tabernacle. "The priest who offers it for sin shall eat it. In a holy place it shall be eaten, in the court of the tabernacle of meeting. Everyone who touches its flesh must be holy. . . . All the males among the priests may eat it. It is most holy" (Leviticus 6:26–27, 29).

The sin offering didn't just involve the shedding of blood; it also involved the eating of the sacrifice. The same sacrifice that was offered for the remission of sins became holy food for the priests of God. This might all be quite unfamiliar for us, but it was very familiar to the disciples in the Upper Room and to the first congregations to celebrate the Lord's Supper. When Jesus said this is His blood shed for us for the remission of sins, He was telling us that He is our sin offering and inviting us as His "royal priesthood" (1 Peter 2:9)—those whom He has made "kings and priests to our God" (Revelation 5:10)—to eat Him as our most holy food.

But He also invites us to drink His blood. The Old Testament priests were never allowed to do that (see Leviticus 17:10–12). The blood of the sin offering was only sprinkled and poured; it was never drunk. But when it was poured out, it was poured out in the same place as something else: wine (see Numbers 28:7).[1] Neither the blood nor the wine (see Leviticus 10:9) were to be drunk; both were to be poured out. The poured-out blood of the sin offerings and the poured-out wine of drink offerings flowed and mixed together at the base of God's altar. And now, the blood of Christ, our sin offering, flows to us through the wine of the cup of the Lord's Supper.

Blood and wine have always been joined in the worship of God. In the worship of the Tabernacle, the blood and the wine belonged exclusively to the Lord. But now, as we worship at the Lord's table, He shares His blood and wine with us.

Christ has given Himself for us as the ultimate and true sin offering. That points us to how our sins are forgiven through His death in our place. But it also points us to His invitation to eat His body and drink His blood. When Jesus said, "This is My blood of the new covenant, which is shed for many for the remission of sins" (Matthew 26:28), He wasn't holding out a blood-smeared fragment of the wood of the cross, but the cup of the Lord's Supper.

Jesus' death on the cross has accomplished something astonishingly powerful: the remission of sins. But Jesus doesn't simply offer us something He has accomplished for us, although that would be wonderful enough. He gives us something much better. Jesus gives us Himself. So we don't only have forgiveness; we have Christ for our sin offering. And week by week, each time we come to His table, we feed upon the most holy food of the perfect once-for-all sin offering, and taste of the remission of sins as we taste afresh of our gracious and glorious Savior.

THE CUP OF GOD'S WRATH

At the supper, Jesus took the cup. Scripture doesn't simply tell us that He took wine. It's always "the cup" (see Matthew 26:27; Mark 14:23; Luke 22:20; 1 Corinthians 10:16, 21; 11:25–26). The Bible places a significance on the cup, so we need to be careful to avoid replacing "cup" with "wine." Every word of Scripture is inspired by God; if He has chosen the word "cup" rather than the word "wine," it is important.

If we don't unintentionally switch the word in our minds as we read, we'll see the connection with what happens after the Last Supper, when Jesus and the disciples go to the Garden of Gethsemane. There Jesus speaks again of the cup as He prays to the Father: "O My Father, if it is possible, let this cup pass from Me; nevertheless, not as I will, but as You will. . . . O My Father, if this cup cannot pass away from Me unless I drink it, Your will be done" (Matthew 26:39, 42; see also Mark 14:36; Luke 22:42). In Matthew, Mark and Luke's gospels, this prayer comes only a few verses after Jesus' words of institution for the supper. Reading straight through, we can hardly avoid noticing the echo of the cup. We have a cup in the Upper Room for us to drink, and a cup in the Garden for Jesus to drink (see John 18:11).

Yet Gethsemane isn't the first time that Jesus spoke of a cup He was going to drink. Shortly before arriving in Jerusalem on Palm Sunday, the mother of James and John had come to the Lord, asking for her two sons to have the privilege of sitting at His right and left in the coming Kingdom. In His answer, Jesus spoke of the cup to James and John: "You do not know what you ask. Are you able to drink the cup that I am about to drink, and be baptized with the baptism that I am baptized with?" (Matthew 20:22; Mark 10:38).

Jesus connects this cup with a baptism. Both this cup and this baptism are yet to be realized. It's the baptism He speaks of in Luke 12:50, when He says, "I have a baptism to be baptized with, and how distressed I am till it is accomplished!"

When James and John's mother came to put this question about her sons to Jesus, the Lord had just spoken of this baptism and cup in another way: "Behold, we are going up to Jerusalem, and the Son of Man will be betrayed to the chief priests and to the scribes; and they will condemn Him to death, and deliver Him to the Gentiles to mock and to scourge and to crucify. And the third day He will rise again" (Matthew 20:18–19).

It's in His crucifixion—in His death on the cross—that Jesus would drink the cup and be baptized with this baptism. But there is another cup the Scriptures had long foretold: the "wine cup of fury" from the hand of the Lord (Jeremiah 25:15; see also Jeremiah 49:12). This cup Jesus would drink on the cross is not the physical suffering of crucifixion; it is the cup of God's wrath that we deserved for our sins. Through His atoning death in our place, Jesus has drunk it to the dregs for us.

> Mine is the sin, but Thine the righteousness;
> mine is the guilt, but Thine the cleansing blood;
> here is my robe, my refuge, and my peace—
> Thy blood, Thy righteousness, O Lord, my God.[2]

At the cross, Jesus has taken our place in bearing our judgment. He has drained the cup of God's wrath so that we can drink of the cup of salvation, as we call upon the name of our Lord (see Psalm 116:13). At the cross, He has taken our place as our great sin offering. And now, we're welcomed as God's priests to eat the most holy food as we come and feed upon Christ in the supper.

> Here would I feed upon the bread of God,
> here drink with Thee the royal wine of heaven;
> here would I lay aside each earthly load,
> here taste afresh the calm of sin forgiven.[3]

At the table we proclaim the Lord's death, as we eat of Christ who is our sin offering and our Passover Lamb. And at the table we proclaim the Lord's death as we drink the cup of the fruit of the True Vine (see John 15:1).

IN REMEMBRANCE OF ME

Now, maybe you've been wondering when I would get to Jesus' words, "This do in remembrance of Me"? Isn't He telling us that the supper is just something to remind us of His death? Well, only if you read the word *remembrance* in a modern way. We should be reading it in a biblical way. Scripture interprets Scripture, so let's look at what Scripture has to say about remembrance.

Christ is our Passover who "was sacrificed for us," and as a result we now "keep the feast" (1 Corinthians 5:7–8). When we partake of Christ in the supper, we feed upon our true Passover Lamb.

From the time of Moses to the time of Jesus, a memorial was kept every year at Passover (see Exodus 12:14). The word translated *memorial* in English in the Old Testament could equally be translated as *a remembrance*. The Passover Feast wasn't just something to help people remember what had happened a long time ago; it was a powerful proclamation of God's mighty deliverance of His people.

The Passover isn't the only memorial we find in the Old Testament. The other memorials show us that they often act as a remembrance in the opposite direction. In Leviticus, we see that in the sacrifices of the Tabernacle, memorials are sent up *to the Lord*! (Leviticus 2:2, 9, 16; 5:12; 6:15). Jesus didn't say, "Do this so that *you* will remember Me." A memorial has a much richer and deeper biblical meaning than just an object lesson to jog our memory. Christ in the supper is our memorial both in the powerful proclamation of His death to us, and in the proclamation of His death as a memorial before God for us! As we eat and drink at the Lord's table, God keeps on seeing what He has done for us in Jesus. (It's not that He ever forgets. It's like carrying a photo or memento in our wallet of someone or some event that is precious to us, so we'll have it with us wherever we go.) Christ in the supper is also our memorial in the powerful proclamation of His promised return, for we proclaim the Lord's death only until He comes.

As a memorial, the Lord's Supper takes us back to Calvary and forward to the Lord's return, when we will feast with Him forever. And it doesn't *just* remind us of Calvary and of the promise of Christ's coming; it takes us there. At the table, we partake of the sacrifice of the cross, and as we do so, the Holy Spirit gives us a foretaste of the feast to come. Past, present and future meet at the Lord's table, for in the supper, heaven meets earth. How? Because Jesus Himself is present in this memorial.

OUR ONE PRIEST
AND OUR ONE SACRIFICE

Christ offered Himself up on the cross once-for-all as our perfect, atoning sacrifice. And so, in the Lord's Supper, we can't make a new offering. We can't repeat Christ's sacrifice; "it is finished!" (John 19:30).

But now in heaven as our great High Priest, the Lord Jesus intercedes for us by pleading the blood He shed as a sacrifice in our place (Hebrews 7:25; Romans 8:34). Christ's finished sacrifice and His abiding intercession go together, and they can't be separated. So when we gather 'round the Lord's table for this memorial meal, the memorial doesn't just connect us to Christ's cross and Christ's coming, but also to His intercession for us in heaven now. We join with our great High Priest when we come to the table, not to plead in our own right, but as we feed upon Him in the supper, we're joined to the One who truly pleads His blood for us at the table. Jesus presents the atonement to the Father in the power of the Holy Spirit. And because by His body and blood He abides in us and we abide in Him (John 6:56), in Him we plead the blood as we drink of the cup in the supper.

Jesus is the only One who can present that finished sacrifice to the Father, but we are united to Jesus, who presents His sacrifice for us. Only in Jesus and through Jesus can we, by the Holy Spirit, plead the blood in the breaking of bread. At the table, in our communion with Christ's body and blood, we partake of that once-for-all sacrifice of the cross that Jesus, our great High Priest, is now presenting for us in heaven. So this bread and wine, the cross and the heavenly Holy of Holies are all united at the table of remembrance as we proclaim the Lord's death.

4

Holy Ground

THERE ARE FEW PEOPLE in the Old Testament who encountered the presence of the Lord in the powerful way that the prophet Isaiah did in the year that King Uzziah died. It's such a precious and powerful account that, through the centuries, the Church has continued to come back to it to see what it is like to encounter the Lord in His glory and grace. Since the earliest days, all over the world, on every continent, in probably every language to which the Gospel has spread, many Christians raise their voices each time they gather at the Lord's table with words taken from Isaiah 6. They join the angels and archangels in proclaiming, "Holy, holy, holy" to our Lord God of hosts (Isaiah 6:3).[1]

"Holy, holy, holy" is the song of the angels. Isaiah catches a glimpse of the seraphim as they raise this song, and later

John sees them still singing those same three words when he witnesses the worship of heaven in Revelation 4. And as they sing, even the seraphim veil their faces in the presence of the Thrice-Holy God (Isaiah 6:2). The *holy* angels veil their faces as they proclaim the holiness of the Lord! They have never sinned, and yet they cover their eyes before the holy presence of God. They veil their faces, because they are not fit to look upon the Holy One of Israel. They veil their feet, because they are on holy ground in the presence of the Lord, where even they are not fit to set foot. The holy angels proclaim and magnify the holiness of the Holy God alone.

The Lord of Hosts is majestic in holiness. Even the holy angels cannot compare to the holiness of God. He is incomparable. Moses and the children of Israel acknowledged it when they sang after He parted the waters of the Red Sea and led them through on dry ground: "Who is like You, O LORD, among the gods? Who is like You, glorious in holiness, fearful in praises, doing wonders?" (Exodus 15:11). Hannah proclaimed it too: "No one is holy like the LORD, for there is none besides You, nor is there any rock like our God" (1 Samuel 2:2). Nothing and no one can compare to the Lord our God in His holiness. His holiness sets Him apart from everything else, and even the glorified saints in heaven and the sinless angels of glory, holy as they are, marvel at the incomparable holiness of their God.

But if the holy angels and the glorified saints in heaven marvel at the holiness of the Lord, then what happens to His people on earth when they encounter the Lord in the beauty of holiness? Well, what happened to the holy prophet Isaiah?

HOLINESS AND SINFULNESS

The heavenly host sang their hymn of praise to the Thrice-Holy God, yet Isaiah himself did not join in that song. He heard the song of the seraphim, and he felt the posts of the door shaken by the sound (Isaiah 6:4), as he beheld "the LORD sitting on a throne, high and lifted up, and the train of His robe filled the temple" (Isaiah 6:1). The sight was glorious. The sight was Jesus (John 12:41). But as glorious as the sight of our Savior is, Isaiah's first reaction wasn't to burst into songs of joy. No, the first thing Isaiah did was to say, "Woe is me, for I am undone!" (Isaiah 6:5).

As Isaiah shows us, seeing the Lord in His glory means we can't help but see ourselves as we really are. The dazzling perfection of the Lord shows our imperfection. The radiant purity of the Lord opens our eyes to our impurity.

Now, Isaiah isn't some terrible criminal who has somehow wandered into the Temple—Isaiah is already God's prophet! He has already been proclaiming God's holy Word. And yet the holy prophet, when he receives a glimpse of the holiness of the Lord, discovers that he stands before Him as a sinner. The prophet who has spoken the Lord's pure Word discovers that he is yet "a man of unclean lips" (Isaiah 6:5). By our standards, Isaiah is an incredibly holy man, yet in the presence of the Lord we see that none of us can lay hold to any merit of our own. "If we say that we have no sin, we deceive ourselves, and the truth is not in us" (1 John 1:8).

But this is not a gloomy message. For "Christ Jesus came into the world to save sinners" (1 Timothy 1:15), and only sinners. As Jesus Himself put it, "Those who are well have no need of a physician, but those who are sick. I did not come to call the righteous, but sinners, to repentance" (Mark 2:17). Seeing our sinfulness is not a bad thing at all; it's a necessary thing. For only those who see their sin can repent of their sin. Only those who see their sinfulness know their neediness. Only those who see their impurity see their need of Christ's purity.

The Lord is not waiting for us to find a way to cleanse *ourselves* of our sinfulness before we approach Him. If that were the case, no one would ever come. Instead, He is the God who calls sinners. And He is the God who forgives and cleanses sinners; who, by His Holy Spirit, convicts us of our sins and draws us to Jesus, the Savior of Sinners, in repentance and faith. He is the God who, when we "were dead in trespasses and sins . . . made us alive together with Christ (by grace you have been saved)" (Ephesians 2:1, 5). When we feel the depths of our sin, we can pray with the psalmist: "If You, LORD, should mark iniquities, O Lord, who could stand? But there is forgiveness with You, that You may be feared" (Psalm 130:3–4).

Isaiah knew both the fear of the Lord and the forgiveness of the Lord. The Lord invites us to come and experience both in His presence as well.

RUNNING IN THE RIGHT DIRECTION

Christians still sin. We have not yet been glorified. One day, when we are gathered with the saints in glory, we will no longer sin. But until that day, as we live in this in-between time of our pilgrimage on earth, sin still haunts us. And as we grow in grace and maturity, we see more of our sinfulness. It's not that we are suddenly becoming more sinful, but rather, as we see more and more of the glory and greatness—of the holiness, purity and perfection—of the Lord we love, the radiant brilliance of His light opens our eyes to sin in our lives that we hadn't noticed before. Maturity in the Christian life doesn't look like never sinning; it looks like mourning our sins and confessing our sins. (It also looks like killing the sin, but we'll look at that in a later chapter.) It looks like the holy prophet Isaiah, falling down immediately in the presence of the Lord to acknowledge our sin and our need of His forgiveness and cleansing.

One of the biggest questions in the Christian life is, How do you deal with sin? And really, there are only two options: Either we run to Jesus when we sin, or we run away from Jesus when we sin. (We sometimes like to trick ourselves into thinking there's a third option—pausing—but that's really just a disguised way of running away.)

We learn this right at the very beginning, in the Garden of Eden. When Adam and Eve sinned, "They heard the sound of the LORD God walking in the garden in the cool of the day, and Adam and his wife hid themselves from the presence of the LORD God among the trees of the garden" (Genesis 3:8). After sinning, Adam and Eve felt unworthy to stand in the presence of the Lord. They were guilty, and they knew it. So they decided to avoid the Lord's presence. They thought they would pause, and not see the Lord right now (our imaginary third option). But in order to do that, they had to run away and hide. When the Lord asked Adam where he was, Adam explained: "I heard Your voice in the garden, and I was afraid because I was naked; and I hid myself" (Genesis 3:10). Instead of a good fear of the Lord that would bring him to the Lord for forgiveness, Adam had a bad fear of the Lord that made him run away from Him and hide.

And that's the choice we all face each time we sin. We can run away from the Lord, or we can run to the Savior for His forgiveness and cleansing. Will we be like Adam and hide? Or will we be like Isaiah and confess our sin?

Now, maybe you are thinking that if even the sinless seraphim veiled their faces in God's presence, how could you possibly look upon the Lord when you've sinned? Maybe you want to say that because God is "of purer eyes than to behold evil, and cannot look on wickedness" (Habakkuk 1:13), how could you possibly come anywhere near Him when you've committed some transgression? You feel the need to hide for a few days or a few weeks until you feel less guilty before you come and ask for His forgiveness.

Well, let me point out that the seraphim veil their eyes, but they don't flee from His presence. And yes, the Lord is of purer eyes than to behold evil, but He's not of purer eyes than to forgive it (Micah 7:18). Time doesn't remove guilt. Your *feelings* of guiltiness and shame might diminish with time, but it's only your feelings that are changing. Nothing has changed before God. And nothing will, until you stop running *from* Him and run *to* Him. There is forgiveness with Him, that He may be feared (the good and godly sort of fear). Running away and hiding is never a solution to sin. The only solution is to run to the Savior and receive His mercy and forgiveness. That invitation to run to Him is always open to us, but it's proclaimed afresh to us each time we come to the Lord's table.

WHAT DOES IT MEAN TO "EXAMINE YOURSELF"?

After some late lectures one evening, I sat down for dinner in the college dining hall. Because I had been teaching those late classes, I hadn't been able to go to the breaking of bread we held in the chapel each day before dinner. So someone else had led it in my place. As I sat down to eat, some of the students started talking about the Communion service I'd just missed.

"It was a good service," they said, "but we didn't do that thing you always do."

"What thing's that?" I asked.

"We didn't stop for a while to examine ourselves."

I was a bit surprised that they thought of taking time to examine themselves before coming to the Lord's table as "that thing I always did." For me, I'd always grown up with that as an essential part of the breaking of bread. But as I talked to my students, I discovered that many of them had never experienced that part of the service before. As the supper has been pushed aside from its central place in worship, in many places it has been trimmed down to take less time. As a result, examining ourselves and confessing our sins has disappeared. Now, it's true that examining ourselves would benefit from more time than just a few minutes before Communion on a Sunday morning. Christians of previous generations used to take time the night before Communion and then that morning before coming to church to examine and prepare themselves. And we'd be wise to follow their example. But those few minutes in the service remind us that we need to prepare and examine ourselves.

Why do we need this self-examination? Because the Bible tells us to examine ourselves before we eat and drink of the Lord's Supper (see 1 Corinthians 11:28). But what does that mean?

Well, let's start first with what it doesn't mean. It doesn't mean to try to figure out whether you've been good enough to come to the Lord's table. Sometimes that's the idea people get. And then they get scared to come and receive Communion. They want to let the bread and the cup pass them by, just in case. Now, it's true that there is a strong warning in the Scripture, but let's look at what it actually says.

> Therefore whoever eats this bread or drinks this cup of the Lord in an unworthy manner will be guilty of the body and blood of the Lord. But let a man examine himself, and so let him eat of the bread and drink of the cup. For he who eats and drinks in an unworthy manner eats and drinks judgment to himself, not discerning the Lord's body. For this reason many are weak and sick among you, and many sleep. For if we would judge ourselves, we would not be judged. But when we are judged, we are chastened by the Lord, that we may not be condemned with the world.
>
> 1 Corinthians 11:27–32

Eating and drinking unworthily is very serious indeed. Those who eat and drink unworthily are guilty of Christ's body and blood. They eat and drink judgment to themselves, and it can even lead to sickness and death. (Death is what Paul's getting at with "and many sleep"—they're not napping; they've died.) No wonder some people are scared to take Communion!

But notice what Paul writes in the middle of that passage: "Let a man examine himself, and *so let him eat of the bread and drink of the cup*" (1 Corinthians 11:28, emphasis added). The call to self-examination isn't a barrier to coming to the table; it's an invitation. We're not called to examine ourselves to see whether we *should* eat and drink, but to eat and drink with confidence in the Savior's forgiveness!

The invitation to examine ourselves and then eat is an invitation to run to Jesus, not to run away from Him. By calling us to examine ourselves, Jesus is reaching out His nail-scarred hands to us in love, to draw us back to Him for forgiveness, for cleansing, for restoration, for transformation and to welcome us into His loving embrace at the table.

At the table, we see the Lord, high and lifted up. You might not realize it, but we do. We don't physically see the Lord's body in the supper; we see only the bread. By faith we discern that it isn't merely bread anymore. This "bread that we break, is . . . a participation in the body of Christ," just as "the cup of blessing that we bless, is . . . a participation in the blood of Christ" (1 Corinthians 10:16 ESV). With our physical eyes, we see the bread and wine; but with the eyes of faith we discern Christ's body and blood. And so, with the eyes of faith, we see Jesus, high and lifted up in the breaking of bread. Just as Isaiah saw Jesus high and lifted up in the Temple. And like Isaiah, seeing the exalted Lord should cause us to bow down and confess our sins.

Twice Isaiah uses this expression to speak of Jesus. In Isaiah 6:1, the prophet sees the Lord "high and lifted up" with His glory filling the Temple. Then in Isaiah 52, he writes again of Jesus "high and lifted up" (verse 13 ESV) as the One whose "visage was marred more than any man" (verse 14). He is lifted up as "a Man of sorrows and acquainted with grief" (Isaiah 53:3) who:

> has borne our griefs
> and carried our sorrows;
> yet we esteemed Him stricken,
> smitten by God, and afflicted.
> But He was wounded for our transgressions,
> He was bruised for our iniquities;
> the chastisement for our peace was upon Him,
> and by His stripes we are healed.
> All we like sheep have gone astray;
> we have turned, every one, to his own way;
> and the LORD has laid on Him the iniquity of us all.
>
> Isaiah 53:4–6

The One who was high and lifted up in the glory-filled Temple is the same One who was high and lifted up in our place on the cross of Calvary. The cross is where we find the glory of the Lord. And the supper is where we find the cross, as we encounter our Savior in His body given for us and His blood shed for us. Jesus is high and lifted up at the Lord's table as the glorious Lord who reigns through His cross, and whose glory fills His Temple (—which is now us, His body!).

This is the powerful, glorious, resplendent Lord whom we encounter in the supper—the Lord who offered Himself up for us on the cross. We encounter His holy presence, drawing near to the bread and wine where He makes Himself known (as Moses drew near to the burning bush), recognizing that we are on holy ground. By faith, we see Him, as Isaiah did, high and lifted up, and in His light we see our sin and our need for His mercy and forgiveness—our need for Him. And that glorious and gracious sight causes us to fall to our knees in repentance and confession, in reverence and awe. At the sight of the Holy Crucified One, high and lifted up in His glory for us, we fall down to "worship the LORD in the beauty of holiness.... And in His temple everyone says, 'Glory!'" (Psalm 29:2, 9).

So the most important question we can ask as we examine ourselves before we come to the table is, *Am I trusting in this Jesus, the glorious and gracious Savior who was lifted up on the cross for me and invites me to meet Him at His table?* Andrew Murray, the great South African saint, said, "Self-examination is simple": Either you're in Christ (and He's in you) or you aren't. "There is no third condition. The life of Christ in you may still be weak, but if you are truly born again and a child of God, Christ is in you. And then, as a child you have access to the table of the Father and a share in the children's bread."[2]

Receiving the supper worthily doesn't mean we've done something worthy (or avoided doing something unworthy). Worthiness is found only through faith in Jesus. Martin Luther put it like this: "That person is truly worthy and well prepared who has faith in these words: 'Given and shed for you for the forgiveness of sins.' But whoever does not believe these words or doubts them is unworthy and ill-prepared, for the words 'For you' require nothing but believing hearts."[3]

But if you're still tempted to run and hide (or let the bread and cup pass you by), Dr. Luther has some words for you too:

Those who [recognize] their weakness, desire to be rid of it and long for help, should regard and use [the supper] as a precious antidote against the poison which they have in them. For here in the Sacrament you are to receive from the lips of Christ forgiveness of sin, which contains and brings with it the grace of God and the Spirit with all His gifts, protection, shelter, and power against death and the devil and all misfortune. . . . If, therefore, you are heavy-laden and feel your weakness, then go joyfully to this Sacrament and obtain refreshment, consolation, and strength. For if you would wait until you are rid of such burdens, that you might come to the Sacrament pure and worthy, you must forever stay away.[4]

In other words, run to the blood shed for you for the remission of sins; don't run away from it. Run to Jesus, and taste afresh of His forgiveness and the joy of His salvation.

Those who eat and drink worthily at the Lord's table aren't those who are full of confidence in their own goodness. We're not saved by our good works; we're saved only by God's grace in Jesus. And we don't come to the table by our good works; we come only by God's grace to us in Jesus. Those who eat and drink worthily are those who come with what the Puritan William Bradshaw called "a holy appetite . . . a spiritual hungering and thirsting after Christ Jesus and His merits." And that holy appetite arises "from a sense of the weakness of our faith and repentance, and a desire to have them strengthened."[5] Those who eat and drink worthily are those who recognize their weakness and their need and who run to Jesus for refuge.

REPENTANCE

Running to Jesus is repentant running. Examining ourselves isn't about making a list of our sins to keep us away from the table. But in examining ourselves, we recognize our sins and run to Christ with them to confess. For He has promised in His Word that "if we confess our sins, He is faithful and just to forgive us our sins and to cleanse us from all unrighteousness" (1 John 1:9). Examining ourselves and confessing our sins go together, because confessing our sins is what running to Jesus looks like.

But confessing our sins is not merely listing them. Forgiveness doesn't come by merely inserting the name of our sin into a prepackaged prayer. Forgiveness isn't found in the form of words, but in the God of grace. So true confession isn't just words on our lips, but a prayer that springs from a pierced heart and lays hold of a gracious God. True confession is a heartfelt cry of repentance, as, hating our sins, we turn from them to our faithful and just Savior.

First, we need to see our sins. We so often hide them from ourselves. We get used to them and they become invisible to us. But the Holy Spirit opens our eyes to convict us of sin (John 16:8). Suddenly, by His Spirit, God puts His finger on something and points it out as sinful. He does that in all sorts of ways. Sometimes it's as we're reading the Bible. Sometimes while we pray. Sometimes as we spend time with other Christians. Sometimes we're just suddenly struck by conviction as we go about our day. But whatever way the Spirit brings conviction, we need to respond to it with sorrow.

That's the next step: sorrow for sin. Godly sorrow for sin isn't just a momentary twinge of sadness. The Bible calls it "a broken and a contrite heart" (Psalm 51:17). We see our sin for what it really is, and we grieve over our sinfulness. As the Holy Spirit convicts us of sin, He turns our hearts against it. We see our sin and we hate it, and our heart is broken that we have so grieved our holy God.

This seeing and sorrowing over sin leads us to truly confess our sins. Flowing out of a heart grieving over its sin, confession cannot be merely a list. It's something much more powerful: It's an accusation—an accusation against ourselves! When the prophet Nathan confronted David over his sin, the Lord opened the king's eyes to the reality of his guilt. First Nathan accused David (see 2 Samuel 12:7), but that gave way to David accusing himself:

> For I acknowledge my transgressions, and my sin is always before me. Against You, You only, have I sinned, and done this evil in Your sight—that You may be found just when You speak, and blameless when You judge.
>
> Psalm 51:3–4

Our sorrow over sin flows over into self-accusation as we confess our sins and our sinfulness to the Lord. That might sound quite negative, but in reality, it is a very positive thing indeed. As the great Puritan Thomas Watson explained, "The truth is that by this self-accusing we prevent Satan's accusing."[6] That's who Satan is: the accuser, who seeks to accuse us before God night and day (see Revelation 12:10). But in humbling ourselves before our holy God, and accusing ourselves while clinging to His mercy in confessing our sins, the devil's accusing power is taken away. So when Satan brings his accusations, he has no case; his accusations come too late.

True confession is heartfelt confession. "Our hearts must go along with our confessions," as Thomas Watson put it.[7] We can't truly confess a sin we love. True confession bursts out as we come to hate our sins, as we begin to catch a glimpse of how our holy God sees them. In confession we're not merely lamenting sin in general. We're not saying, "Oh, I suppose I must have sinned, so, sorry about that." No! When David repented after having Uriah the Hittite killed, he confessed "the guilt of bloodshed" (Psalm 51:14). If confession flows from seeing our sins and sorrowing over them, then it's about particular sins—sins we see, sins that break our hearts.

But true confession also goes deeper than particular sins. David not only confessed his bloodshed, but his sinfulness and need for a clean heart and transformation deep within:

> Behold, I was brought forth in iniquity, and in sin my mother conceived me. Behold, You desire truth in the inward parts, and in the hidden part You will make me to know wisdom. . . . Create in me a clean heart, O God, and renew a steadfast spirit within me.
>
> Psalm 51:5–6, 10

Sin isn't just bad things we do. Sin goes deep down into our fallen nature. Like David, we were born with a sinful nature. And even now as believers, although Jesus has freed us from sin's dominion so that it no longer has the power it once had, there is still sin that dwells in us (see Romans 7:17). We are still waiting for that final day of full redemption when Jesus raises us to glorious, sinless, resurrection life. For now, there is still an enemy of evil within, and the sinful deeds we do are symptoms of that indwelling sin deep down within. Mark Jones paints a vivid picture to help us understand: "A Trojan horse remains in our heart, with enemies inside ready to pounce."[8]

David's great prayer of repentance in Psalm 51 shows us that this Trojan horse isn't something that excuses our sins.

We can't brush off our sinful thoughts and deeds as inevitable and insignificant because there's a sinful nature within. Rather, we should confess this fountain of sin within. Johann Gerhard, a mighty servant of God in Germany after the Reformation, wrote that the godly repent and confess not only of the sinful deeds they commit, "but also of the fount of all actual sins, namely the original stain; not only outward sins, but also the inner corruption."[9] The inner corruption should bother us. It certainly shouldn't control us. Jesus has paid the price to set us free from sin's dominion by dying on the cross for our sin. So, rather than getting entangled back up in the tentacles of that dying monster, we should lament its presence and confess our sinfulness, until the day of full redemption (Ephesians 1:14; 4:30).

Examining ourselves doesn't mean making a list of our sins to see if we've been good enough to come to the table. It means confessing our sins and running to meet with our Savior from sin at the table.

HOLY HUMILITY

As we approach the Lord's table, see the Savior high and lifted up and fall down to confess our sins, we are humbled. And being humbled is always a good thing. For it is the humble whom the Lord will beautify with salvation (see Psalm 149:4). It is the humble whom the Lord lifts up (see Psalm 147:6). It is the humble to whom the Lord gives grace (see Proverbs 3:34).

The Holy One who is high and lifted up dwells with the humble. "For thus says the High and Lofty One who inhabits eternity, whose name is Holy: 'I dwell in the high and holy place, with him who has a contrite and humble spirit, to revive the spirit of the humble'" (Isaiah 57:15). We come to the Holy One who is high and lifted up when we come to the breaking of bread. Confessing our sins, we come to Him humbly. And in that way, Jesus' promise will be fulfilled: "He that eats my flesh and drinks my blood dwells in me and I in him" (John 6:56 DARBY). As we come humbly to the supper to feed on our Savior, the high and lofty One whose name is holy dwells in His humble people by His body and blood.

The only way into the presence of the Lord is the way of humility. That's what Isaiah discovered in a very powerful way in the year that King Uzziah died. And that insight led Thomas Cranmer, one of the Protestant Reformers, to write one of the greatest prayers of all time, outside the Bible: the Prayer of Humble Access, for the congregation to pray before coming to eat and drink the Lord's Supper.

> We do not presume to come to this your table, merciful Lord, trusting in our own righteousness but in your manifold and great mercies. We are not worthy so much as to gather up the crumbs under your table. But you are the same Lord, whose nature is always to have mercy. Grant us, therefore, gracious Lord, so to eat the flesh of your dear Son Jesus Christ, and to drink his blood, that our sinful bodies may be made clean by his body, and our souls washed through his most precious blood, and that we may evermore dwell in him and he in us. Amen.[10]

We don't presume as we come to the Lord's table; instead, we come humbly, confessing our sins and our sinfulness, and entrusting ourselves only to our gracious God's great and abundant mercy. We admit that, in ourselves, we're not worthy even to gather up crumbs, but that recognition is the only way we can eat and drink worthily. So we come, trusting in Jesus' promise that whoever eats His flesh and drinks His blood dwells in Him and He in them, as we come humbly to the One who dwells with the humble.

5

One Bread, One Body

HAVE A LOOK AROUND YOU in church on Sunday. Who's there? I don't mean look to see who's missing. I mean look and see all the very different people who are sitting around you in church. As the bread is broken, look and see all the people with whom you're sharing that loaf, who aren't at all like you. As the cup is passed to you, look and see all the glorious variety of people who've drunk from it too. The Church is filled with people of all ages, backgrounds, ethnicities, social groups, opinions, classes and cultures. Even if you live in the middle of nowhere, there are probably a lot of people in your church whom you wouldn't be sitting in a room with if it wasn't for Jesus. Because Jesus is the One who holds the Church together. He's the One who unites us. He's the one thing we all have in common.

There might be some people in your church whom you'd share a meal with, even if you weren't believers. But undoubtedly, not all of them. And yet, this group of people whom the world would never imagine finding in the same place, never mind around the same table, share a meal week after week as we gather for the Lord's Supper. At the Lord's table, this new family shares the richest of feasts.

I grew up in Northern Ireland at the end of the Troubles. It was a country that was very divided. People from the two communities—Protestant and Catholic—went to different schools and lived on different streets, if not in different towns or villages. A lot of people didn't really know many from the other community. Yet, every Lord's Day, I would see people from Protestant families and people from Catholic families sit around the Lord's table together in our little Pentecostal church and eat and drink in the presence of the Lord. And flowing out of that unity in the Lord's Supper, people ate and drank together—and visited and babysat and helped in all sorts of ways—in parts of the city they'd never normally have set foot in, because they belonged to "the other side." At a time when terrorist attacks were still going on between the two communities, the dividing wall between them was torn down because of Jesus, and that was never more evident than when we all ate and drank together as one family at the Lord's table.

COMMUNION AND FELLOWSHIP

We sometimes use words in funny ways. In English, *fellowship* and *communion* sound like two quite different things, yet they translate the same Greek word. Fellowship and communion are the same thing: You can't have fellowship without communion, and you can't have communion without fellowship. So fellowship with our brothers and sisters in the Church is communion with them. And communion with Christ is fellowship with Him. The two belong together.

John writes about this at the beginning of his first letter:

> That which was from the beginning, which we have heard, which we have seen with our eyes, which we have looked upon, and our hands have handled, concerning the Word of life—the life was manifested, and we have seen, and bear witness, and declare to you that eternal life which was with the Father and was manifested to us—that which we have seen and heard we declare to you, that you also may have fellowship with us; and truly our fellowship is with the Father and with His Son Jesus Christ. And these things we write to you that your joy may be full.
>
> 1 John 1:1–4

John is writing about joy—and we all want joy! But for our joy to be full, John tells us about fellowship. Look around you again in church and see all those very different people with whom you are joined in fellowship. Does that bring you joy? Well, it should! Because John tells us it is only in fellowship that fullness of joy can be found.

Fellowship, you see, has nothing to do with structures or activities. We don't have fellowship because we've stuck a sign over the door renaming the church a "Christian Fellowship." And we don't have it because we all drink a cup of tea after the service on Sunday nights. Fellowship is not created by church signs, cake or cups of coffee. It is created by sharing much more deeply together. And John tells us that our fellowship with one another is rooted first and foremost in our fellowship with the Father and the Son. We have fellowship with one another because of our common fellowship with our God.

But John tells us more than that. This fellowship we have with the Father and the Son, and through them with one another, is a fellowship brought about by the incarnation of Christ. For the sake of this fellowship, John first tells us what "was from the beginning, which we have heard, which we have seen with our eyes, which we have looked upon, and our hands have handled, concerning the Word of life" (1 John 1:1). That's Jesus! He's the Word who was in the beginning with God and is God (see John 1:1–2), and whom John could touch with his hands because He "became flesh and dwelt among us" (John 1:14). John saw and heard and touched the One whose hands uphold the stars and the planets! Those hands, ultimately, would be nailed to the cross for our sake.

John wants to make sure we understand that fellowship does not come through sharing the same ideas or interests, or by sharing the same likes or dislikes. Fellowship comes only through a Person, and that Person is the Lord Jesus Christ, the incarnate Son of God. John emphasizes again in chapter 4 that it is the incarnate God in whom our fellowship is rooted:

> By this you know the Spirit of God: Every spirit that confesses that Jesus Christ has come in the flesh is of God, and every spirit that does not confess that Jesus Christ has come in the flesh is not of God. And this is the spirit of the Antichrist, which you have heard was coming, and is now already in the world.
>
> 1 John 4:2–3

We can talk about God in all sorts of vague ways, but which God are we actually talking about? The God of the Bible is the One who has revealed Himself in Jesus Christ, who came in the flesh. "No one has seen God at any time. The only begotten Son, who is in the bosom of the Father, He has declared Him" (John 1:18). So, if we want to know who God is and what He is like, we need to look at Jesus—God the Son, who has come in our flesh to save us.

The Son became what we are in order to save us. He became a human being like us and lived a truly human life on this earth, with all its joys and sorrows. Why? Well, Irenaeus—a disciple of a disciple of the apostle John—gave a famous pithy answer: Jesus "because of his immeasurable love became what we are in order to make us what he is."[1] Now, that might sound a bit odd, but let's think about it carefully. Who is Jesus? Jesus is the well-beloved Son of the Father. And that's exactly what He makes us. Jesus has saved us and united us to Himself so that we share in all that is His, including His relationship with His Father. So, in Christ, we have been adopted into His Sonship, and that makes us well-beloved sons in the well-beloved Son.

We're all called sons—because it's Jesus' own loving relationship with His Father that we have been brought into. We don't each have a different relationship with the Father; we all share in Christ's. So the Bible calls us all *sons*—men, women, boys and girls—because there aren't different types of children of God. "For you are all sons of God through faith in Christ Jesus. For as many of you as were baptized into Christ have put on Christ. There is neither Jew nor Greek, there is neither slave nor free, there is neither male nor female; for you are all one in Christ Jesus" (Galatians 3:26–28).

As one hymnwriter put it:

> Near, so very near to God,
> I cannot nearer be;
> For, in the Person of His Son,
> I am as near as He.
>
> Dear, so very dear to God,
> More dear I cannot be,
> The love wherewith He loves the Son—
> Such is His love to me.[2]

Jesus took on our flesh and blood and became what we are, so that we could become what He is—so near and so dear and so loved by the Father! In Jesus, we are welcomed into His Father's family. In Jesus, we're anointed in the Anointed One, so we share in His Spirit. And that means we don't have fellowship with Jesus only, but with His Father and His Spirit too. We have fellowship with the Trinity.

That's what John tells us when he writes, "Truly our fellowship is with the Father and with His Son Jesus Christ" (1 John 1:3). If we know the Son, who took on our flesh and blood, we know the Father. In fact, the only way to know the Father is to know the Son. This fellowship with the Father and the Son, and with their Holy Spirit too, is not merely a bonus for some special Christians. This fellowship with the Trinity is the Christian life that we've been saved into. Jesus makes that very clear: "This is eternal life, that they may know You, the only true God, and Jesus Christ whom You have sent" (John 17:3). Being drawn into the love and fellowship of the Trinity is the very nature of eternal life. It is the Christian existence: a loving fellowship with the Father, Son and Holy Spirit.

So what is involved in this loving fellowship with the Trinity? On the night He was betrayed, Jesus prayed to the Father for us, saying, "You . . . have loved them as You have loved Me" (John 17:23). Jesus is speaking about us being in Him and Him being in us—about how we're united together as one with Him. And so, in Him, we share in the very same love the Father has for Jesus. The Father doesn't simply love us like friends of His Son—no! He doesn't have some other, lesser love for us. He embraces us in the love of the Trinity. And so the Holy Spirit pours out the very love of the Triune God in our hearts (see Romans 5:5).

Peter calls this being "partakers of the divine nature" (2 Peter 1:4). That's what true fellowship looks like. Not simply spending a bit of time with God, but partaking of the divine nature. And that word Peter uses for partakers is the Greek word for having communion. Through the incarnation and shed blood of God the Son, we have been brought into communion with the Trinity and have communion with the divine nature. This is our true fellowship with God.

Now, don't get scared. We don't stop being human and start being God. We don't get swallowed up and lose our identity in some notion of "the Divine." It's nothing like that. What is the divine nature? Peter explains a bit more:

His divine power has granted to us all things that pertain to life and godliness, through the knowledge of him who called us to his own glory and excellence, by which he has granted to us his precious and very great promises, so that through them you may become partakers of the divine nature, having escaped from the corruption that is in the world because of sinful desire.

2 Peter 1:3–4 ESV

The Lord has called us to His own glory and excellence. And the Lord has granted us His gracious promises so that we will be partakers of the divine nature. These two aims are one and the same. The divine nature is the glory and excellence of the Triune God. We have been saved to share in the glory of God (see 1 Peter 5:10). We have been saved to share in the divine nature. The Lord has graciously come down to us to lift us up to share (in the way that's possible to us as creatures) in what He is. We have been united to Christ the Son and share in the eternal love between the Father and the Son. We have been filled with the Holy Spirit, and He pours out the love of God in our hearts. So in Jesus and by the Spirit, our life is a life lived in the Trinity. And through the Spirit filling us, the Trinity dwells in us (John 14:16–18, 23).

We share in the divine nature. We share in the glory of the Triune God. But that doesn't mean we share in God's being. We are not turned into God. The other word that Peter uses to describe this goal of God for us helps us to see that more clearly. He calls it God's "excellence" (ESV) or "virtue" (NKJV) (2 Peter 1:3). God is the excellent One who does all things excellently. God is the supremely virtuous One, and all that He does is virtuous and praiseworthy. So if sharing in the divine nature means to share in the excellence or virtue of the Triune God, it involves sharing in His likeness. By being united to the Son, filled with the Spirit and sharing in the Father's eternal love, we are being transformed from glory to glory and conformed to the image of our God. This fellowship—this participation in the divine nature—means both intimacy with the Triune God and transformation by the Triune God. We share in the eternal love between Father, Son and Holy Spirit, and by this almighty, divine love are made more and more like Jesus. Christ is formed in us (see Galatians 4:19). So, to be a partaker of the divine nature means to live in the love of the Trinity and be transformed by that divine, eternal, perfect love.

But this sharing in the divine nature isn't just an individual thing. It's a Church thing. We share together in the divine nature, for we are each united to Jesus and share in communion with God. Peter speaks of us together as "partakers of the divine nature" (2 Peter 1:4). John connects our fellowship with the Father and the Son with our fellowship with one another. "That which we have seen and heard we declare to you, that you also may have fellowship with us; and truly our fellowship is with the Father and with His Son Jesus Christ" (1 John 1:3). See how John links the two. He wants his readers to have fellowship with him, but that fellowship is ultimately rooted in fellowship with the Father and the Son. Our fellowship with one another as Christians relies completely on our mutual fellowship with the Father and the Son in the Spirit.

Our fellowship is with Christ, and then through Him with those who also share in His fellowship. Apart from Jesus there is no real fellowship. Christ is at the center of all true communion. And that means fellowship isn't something we can create. Fellowship is something that is already there at the heart of the Trinity, and we can only be brought into that fellowship by Jesus, who took on our flesh and shed His blood for us. Our fellowship with one another comes down to sharing in the love of Christ. If we have Jesus in common, we have fellowship. And as we grow in Jesus together, we grow in fellowship with one another.

Fellowship isn't ultimately about feelings or actions (although feelings and actions will certainly be involved).

Fellowship is about sharing as Christ's people in the outgoing love of the Triune God. Fellowship is about seeing the overflow of the divine life of love expressed in our ways toward one another, as we respond to the overflowing love of the Trinity. And true fellowship leads to true joy—joy that flows from the Trinity to us (together) in Christ.

But what's all this talk about fellowship got to do with the Lord's Supper? Well, there's a reason we often call the Lord's Supper *Communion*. The supper is the great meeting place between us and Jesus. And, as we've just seen, communion with Christ is intimately linked to communion with Christ's people. We can't separate fellowship with Jesus from fellowship with His Church. The Lord's Supper is never a private devotion. It can't be. It's always a fellowship meal.

GOOD COMMUNION, GOOD RELATIONSHIPS

If communion and fellowship mean the same thing, and if our fellowship with one another flows from our fellowship with Christ, then we can't have bad fellowship and good communion. If we're holding things against people who are coming to the table with us, it's not just between us and them. Even if they're going to the table in a church down the road, that doesn't change things. There is only one Christ upon whom we feed at the table, so even if our Communion tables are in different buildings, cities or continents, we're still coming to the same place. If we want good Communion, we need good fellowship. And good fellowship means good relationships. Jesus warns us about this.

You have heard that it was said to those of old, "You shall not murder, and whoever murders will be in danger of the judgment." But I say to you that whoever is angry with his brother without a cause shall be in danger of the judgment. And whoever says to his brother, "Raca!" shall be in danger of the council. But whoever says, "You fool!" shall be in danger of hell fire. Therefore if you bring your gift to the altar, and there remember that your brother has something against you, leave your gift there before the altar, and go your way. First be reconciled to your brother, and then come and offer your gift.

Matthew 5:21–24

It's not only outward action against our neighbor that matters. Jesus cares about what's happening on the inside. He doesn't want us to merely put on an outward show of niceness or decency. He wants us to have hearts that are open in love to one another. He wants us to live as brothers and sisters who truly love one another (see John 13:34). And love doesn't mean pushing down hatred into the hidden recesses of our hearts. Love means opening our hearts to the Lord, to the Spirit's searching and conviction and to the sprinkling of the blood of Jesus, then opening our hearts to one another in confession, forgiveness and love.

Now, Jesus speaks here of bringing gifts to the altar. These are the sacrifices of the Temple, not the Communion of the Church, so you might be tempted to skip these verses in Matthew and say they have nothing to do with the supper. Rather than skip them, we should pause and think about it: We don't bring gifts to the altar now, we receive gifts at the table, but the gifts we receive—the broken body and shed blood of

Jesus—are the fulfillment of the gifts that were brought to the temple altar. Christ is the once-for-all perfect sacrifice who has fulfilled all the sacrifices of the law. Hebrews tells us that "we have an altar from which those who serve the tabernacle have no right to eat" (Hebrews 13:10). And to our altar the only gift we can bring is ourselves, as we present our "bodies as a living sacrifice, holy and acceptable to God, which is your spiritual worship" (Romans 12:1 ESV). But if we are going to present ourselves—our physical bodies and our whole lives—as a living sacrifice, that involves our relationships. If we insist on holding on to the bitterness of hurts and hatreds instead of letting them be washed away by the healing, cleansing blood of Jesus, then we are not presenting our whole lives and are holding back our spiritual worship. Every day we pray, "Forgive us our trespasses, as we forgive those who trespass against us," and we need to mean it. Broken relationships need to be laid at the foot of the cross, where healing and forgiveness flow.

Now, notice that Jesus doesn't say "if you have something against your brother," but rather "if you ... remember that your brother has something against you" (Matthew 5:23). This isn't a punishment for those who have a grudge; this is grace. The Lord is a reconciling God. He has reconciled us to Himself through the broken body and shed blood of Jesus, and in light of that great reconciliation, He calls us to be reconciled to one another and to be agents of reconciliation. This is God's way of running after us and calling us back to Him and to one another, by sending the person whom we've wronged to us. In this God displays His marvelous grace.

God calls us to great humility. When someone has something against us, our natural feeling is to think that it's their responsibility to sort things out. But God calls us to humble ourselves and, in love, run to the one who has wronged us and seek reconciliation through the power of the blood of Jesus.

This is hard. When people wrong us, it hurts. It's easier to ignore it or leave it until they feel conviction. But the Lord has called us to His own glory and virtue as partakers in the divine nature. He wants His glory, His virtue, His nature to be seen in us: the nature of the God who "when we were enemies" reconciled us to Himself "through the death of His Son" (Romans 5:10); the nature of the Lord who is "gracious and full of compassion" (Psalm 111:4); the nature of Christ who "made Himself of no reputation, taking the form of a bondservant, and coming in the likeness of men . . . humbled Himself and became obedient to the point of death, even the death of the cross" (Philippians 2:7–8).

Alas, even when we humble ourselves and take that faithful and obedient step in love toward the one who has something against us, they may not be willing to reconcile. And there still may be relationships that we find difficult. Yet coming to Jesus at His table can help us grow in love and heal hurts. For each time we come, we remember that we can't come alone. We always come in fellowship with the Church. We always come in fellowship with all those who are in fellowship with Jesus. And that includes the difficult relationships. But we can, in our minds, bring that person to the table with us. Here's a prayer we can pray as we do:

Jesus, I receive You today together with [name the person]. I know we are brothers in You, and I ask Your blessing on [name] today.

Raniero Cantalamessa, who wrote the original prayer that inspired this one, says, "This little act is very pleasing to Jesus because he knows that it causes us to die a little."[3] And as we die to ourselves, Christ's new life of forgiveness, mercy and compassion flows through us.

ONE BREAD, ONE BODY

The Lord's Supper doesn't only give us a chance to restore relationships and improve our fellowship with one another, something much deeper and more powerful is happening as we eat together of the broken bread and blessed cup.

> The cup of blessing which we bless, is it not the communion of the blood of Christ? The bread which we break, is it not the communion of the body of Christ? For we, though many, are one bread and one body; for we all partake of that one bread.
>
> 1 Corinthians 10:16–17

We are being united together as one bread and one body as we eat together of that one bread and drink together of that one cup. When we celebrate the Lord's Supper together, it's not a gathering of individuals who all happen to be having fellowship with Jesus at the same time in the same room—no! Jesus is uniting us together into one body and building us up together in unity in Him, as together—in fellowship with one another—we feed upon our Savior.

When the pandemic hit, churches were thrown into confusion and some introduced things like prepackaged bread and wine for the supper. One of the big problems that creates is that it reinforces the idea of Communion as an individualistic experience. I'm over here in this corner with my bread and wine and you're over there in your corner with yours. We're both eating and drinking at the same time, but there's no connection between what you're eating and drinking and what I'm eating and drinking. I'm having my fellowship with Jesus, and you're having yours.

This is not the biblical picture of the Lord's Supper at all! Jesus passed one loaf and one cup around to His disciples at the Last Supper (and the Church has continued that in most of the world for most of its history). Jesus could very easily have given them each their own small roll of bread and their own cup of wine, but He didn't. Because sharing together in the bread and cup is a very important aspect of Communion. We share in one bread, and we are being built into one body in Christ. We share in one cup and "have all been made to drink into one Spirit" (1 Corinthians 12:13). We share in the same blood and rejoice in the same blood-bought salvation (see Psalm 116:13).

The Communion is not the meal of a small group, a worship team or any other subdivision within the Church. It is the meal of the Church. And so, any time we celebrate the supper, the table should be open to the whole Church. (They don't all have to be there, but they do all need to be invited.) Because we aren't being built up into several different bodies, but one body in Christ. The Lord's Supper is the meal that unites us all. It's not a good idea to take the elements in smaller groups within a big service. We should never be multiple groups holding communion with Christ, but one Church rejoicing in our unity with Christ our Head, and with one another as His body. The supper brings us together and unites us as Christ's Church. As Matthew the Poor says, "When we approach to eat the Body of Christ, each of us approaches as an individual; but after eating, no longer think of yourself as an individual person! You have become a member in the Body. . . . I am united to Him; and so no longer am I just 'me.'"[4]

MISSION'S FUEL AND MISSION'S GOAL

The power of Christ in His supper doesn't end when the service ends. As we encounter the risen Lord at His table, we are energized and empowered for the mission He has given us in the world. We don't linger forever at the table, fearing to go from the place of Christ's presence—not at all! For now that we've eaten and drunk, His presence isn't at the table anymore—it's in us. He feeds us with Himself, and He lives in us. Remember His promise that when we eat His flesh and drink His blood, we dwell in Him and He dwells in us (see John 6:56). We don't just get a brief moment of Christ's presence as we eat and drink; His presence is an abiding presence.

Willie Burton was an early Pentecostal missionary in the Congo who helped plant over two thousand churches. His life was consumed with evangelistic zeal, as he sought to take the Gospel to people who had never heard the name of Jesus. You might think that on his constant pioneering missionary travels he could be forgiven for missing the breaking of bread now and again. But that wouldn't do for Willie Burton. The first day of every week, Willie could be found at the Lord's table. Even when he was traveling by ship between continents, he insisted on holding a Communion service.

In transcontinental railway train or ocean steamer, stretched weak and helpless on a hospital bed, in a dozen countries of three continents, in a vast concourse of over 3,000, or alone with my wife and [one other Christian], encamped in the sombre shade of the Congo forest, we have broken the bread and taken the cup. We would rather miss any meal, or the most important contact rather than miss this.[5]

Look at that! The great missionary evangelist would have rather missed "the most important contact" than miss the Lord's Supper!

Why did he prioritize the supper over everything else? Because he knew that meeting with Jesus in the supper fueled his evangelism.

Can we go to the Breaking of Bread, and whisper in our hearts "Shed for me," unless we face the issue squarely, "Yes, but shed for others too, for the lost all about me, for the heathen in distant lands, shed for the millions who have not even yet heard the Name of the Lord Jesus, or of God's offer of mercy through His crucified and risen Son"?[6]

Every time we hear Christ's words at the table, we remember that He shed His blood "for many for the remission of sins" (Matthew 26:28), not just for us. And He's commissioned us to take that Good News to many too.

It's not only in hearing those words of Jesus that Willie Burton found fuel for mission at the table. He also found it in the vision of Christ in which he was caught up through the breaking of bread.

In those quiet hours of gazing upon our Lord, of recalling His sacrifice for us, we get a vision, a comprehension of that great act of redeeming love. We catch His heart-throb, and see sin and salvation through His eyes. The time is not lost, for we shall now be able to portray Him to others with a more vivid intimacy, a more genuine tenderness, a more powerful assurance than could ever have been possible without it.[7]

This great missionary found empowerment for ever more effective evangelism in meeting with Jesus in the supper. And he was convinced we all should too.

The Church is gathered together as one at the Lord's table. But then from the Lord's table, we're scattered out into the world to take to others that glorious Good News that Jesus' body was broken and His blood was shed not just for us, but for many. At the table we're fed with Christ, and so we go out from the supper filled with Jesus, in the power of the Spirit, to glorify God and make Jesus known.

But that's not the end. Yes, the supper sends us out, fueled for our mission in the world. But the goal of that mission is that others would not only hear of Jesus, but place their trust in Him and be brought into His Body—the Church—where they, too, will eat and drink at the Lord's table.

6

Wonder-Working Power

OUR GOD is a wonder-working God. He's not only the God of miracles, but He's the God who is far beyond all miracles. Even the most incredible of miracles fades away to darkness in the brilliant light of the Lord Himself. By His Word, He spoke the world into being from nothing, "so that the things which are seen were not made of things which are visible" (Hebrews 11:3). He spoke all creation into being, from the stars far above our heads to the grass beneath our feet. He spoke light into the darkness, and order into the chaos. "By the word of the LORD the heavens were made, and all the host of them by the breath of His mouth" (Psalm 33:6). There is nothing our God cannot do, simply by speaking a word.

Yet, the Lord doesn't only speak His Word; He also invites us to come to Him with our words. The wonder-working God, who created the stars and planets, invites us to draw near to Him with our words in prayer. His ear is open to hear us. The way to His throne of grace has been opened up to us by Jesus, our great High Priest. And so, our King and our God invites us, with open arms and open ears, to come boldly and make our needs and requests known to our heavenly Father (see Hebrews 4:14–16; 10:19–23; Matthew 6:9).

Our words do not become magic words. Our words remain weak and faltering, sometimes confused and sometimes mistaken, but our Mediator and Intercessor, Jesus Christ, by His blood and intercession, takes our imperfect words and purifies them and presents them as perfect prayers to our loving Father. We pray like we're praying through Jesus' own mouth.[1] Our prayers, I'm sorry to have to tell you, aren't powerful declarations or decrees; they are expressions of our helplessness and our utter dependence on the Lord. And yet, it's because our prayers flow from our weakness that they are powerful weapons. For "when I am weak, then I am strong" (2 Corinthians 12:10), as the Lord's strength is made perfect in my weakness (see 2 Corinthians 12:9).

The Lord hears our weak words of prayer, and He delights in them. For those are the true words of faith—words that flow from seeing what we cannot do, but our Lord can. Words that flow from knowing that though what I ask is impossible for me, nothing is impossible for Him. Our Lord God has made the heavens and the earth by His great power and His outstretched arm, and nothing is too difficult for Him (see Jeremiah 32:17). He stretches out His arm in response to our prayer (see Acts 4:30).

At the Lord's table we see our weakness. As we behold the Lamb of God who takes away the sin of the world, we are conscious of our sins and of our need for Jesus' precious blood, shed for our forgiveness. As we feed upon the Bread of Heaven, we are conscious of our weakness and our need for Christ to strengthen and sustain us. But at the Lord's table we also hear the glorious promise that what is impossible is not too difficult for our Lord God, as Christ promises us His body and blood. At the Lord's table, we see that our gracious God provides for our needs and responds to our prayer. As in our weakness we cry out for mercy, He meets us with forgiveness and fullness. Our words are weak, but He answers them in wonder-working power. And He does that through speaking His wonder-working Word.

WONDER-WORKING PRAYER

Prayer works wonders, not because our prayers are wonderful, but because our Savior is. He teaches us to pray for wonderful things that He is more than wonderfully able to provide. Sometimes He even teaches us that in ways so ordinary to us, that we've forgotten how big a prayer we're actually praying!

Jesus said, "When you pray, say: Our Father in heaven, hallowed be Your name" (Luke 11:2). That is Jesus' command: When you pray, say these words. Actually, Jesus teaches us the Lord's Prayer twice, and He introduces it in different ways. In Matthew, Jesus tells us, "In this manner, therefore, pray" (Matthew 6:9), while in Luke, He tells us, "When you pray, say" (Luke 11:2). Do you see the difference? In Matthew, He's telling us to pray *like* this—to use the Lord's Prayer as a pattern for our prayers. In Luke, He's telling us to pray *this*—to pray these words themselves, to actually *pray the Lord's Prayer*. In fact, these are the only exact words Jesus ever tells His disciples to pray. The only other words He gives them to use in worship were given on the night He was betrayed: "This is My body . . . this is My blood." That's one reason that a lot of churches pray the Lord's Prayer at Communion—because we're using all the words, together, that Jesus told us to use in worship.

But there's another reason to use the Lord's Prayer during Communion, one you might not have noticed. Have you ever found it strange in the Lord's Prayer that we say, "Give us this day our daily bread" (Matthew 6:11)? Why "this day . . . daily"? If it's "this day" (and we're supposed to be praying this every day), then it already is "daily." So why say both? If you will bear with me for a few moments, I can show you the answer by taking you back to the Greek. In the original language of the New Testament, the word *daily* is a very strange word. It only comes up twice: In Matthew 6:11 and Luke 11:3—both of which are this line of the Lord's Prayer. In fact, it's not just the only place it appears in the Bible; it's the only place it appears anywhere in ancient Greek, apart from one other early Christian book based on the Lord's Prayer. So it seems to be a new word coined specially for the Lord's Prayer!

But why make up a word for "daily'? Greek already had a perfectly good word for it. And yet, neither Matthew nor Luke use it. They both use this brand-new word instead. The reason we tend to translate this brand-new word as "daily" is because the Latin translation uses "daily bread" for the passage in Luke. But even Jerome (who translated the Bible into Latin) wasn't satisfied with just "daily" as a sufficient translation, because he chose another word in Matthew to make sure his readers got a fuller meaning. Over in Matthew, Jerome used (a word we can bring into English as) *supersubstantial*. Now, you can probably see why we use "daily"—*supersubstantial* is not all that great a word for teaching children to say the Lord's Prayer! The word is basically as made up in English as it is in Greek.

But the word is getting at something important: This bread goes beyond (*super*) the normal substance of bread. We're not only praying for the bread we need to sustain us naturally each day, but also the bread that goes beyond natural—we're praying for the supernatural bread. We're praying for physical nourishment and spiritual nourishment. We're praying for the bread on the kitchen table and the bread on the Lord's table: the bread from the oven and the Bread of Heaven. The daily bread we need each day isn't just the food we need to keep us going physically; it's also Jesus, the Bread of Life, who feeds us at His table. Every time we pray the Lord's Prayer, we're not just praying for our physical needs, but our spiritual needs as well. Every time we pray the Lord's Prayer, we're praying to meet with Jesus in the supper. And every time we pray that, it should be stirring up more of that hunger for Him.

Now, we pray this every day, or maybe more. (Before the New Testament was even completed, Christians had been encouraged to pray the Lord's Prayer three times a day, or more.)[2] So, every day we're asking for our daily supernatural bread. Each day we are to pray for a day's supply. We need to constantly be coming to the table to feed upon the Bread of Heaven. We don't ask the Lord for one giant feast to keep us going all year. No. We ask for this heavenly supply a day at a time. This is just like the manna in the Old Testament. Every day in the wilderness, the Lord gave the children of Israel a day's supply of manna. Each day (except the Sabbath), they received their daily bread. And like them, as we await the future feast in the land of our inheritance, the Lord teaches us to ask each day for that day's supply. Every day we need more of Jesus, and every day we should pray for more of Him.

This daily prayer should encourage us to come to the table as often as we can. As John Wesley put it, we have a "duty of constant Communion." He made a passionate plea "that it is the duty of every Christian to receive the Lord's Supper as often as [we] can," because he could see that "the benefits . . . are so great . . . namely, the forgiveness of our past sins and the present strengthening and refreshing of our souls."[3] Those are things we need each and every day, so we should run to the table at every opportunity because Jesus meets us there.

Maybe it sounds hard to pray for supernatural bread each day. We understand ordinary bread much better, and maybe we feel our hunger for it more sharply. We know where ordinary bread comes from, and so maybe it seems like an easier prayer to answer. But don't forget that our prayers don't rely on us; they rely on Jesus. So lift up your eyes to your wonder-working God and see the wonder of what He can do in feeding us each day with our daily Bread of Heaven.

Maybe you've read what I've said about the Lord's presence in the supper, and think it sounds nice, but you just don't know how it could be possible. Well, remember that through our prayers, God works wonders. Jesus Himself has promised that "whatever you ask in My name, that I will do, that the Father may be glorified in the Son. If you ask anything in My name, I will do it" (John 14:13–14). When you long to encounter Christ in the supper, you're longing and praying for something that very much glorifies the Father in the Son. When you pray to meet with Christ at His table, you're praying for what He has promised, and so you're very much praying in His name. So He will do it. "Now this is the confidence that we have in Him, that if we ask anything according to His will, He hears us. And if we know that He hears us, whatever we ask, we know that we have the petitions that we have asked of Him" (1 John 5:14–15). When Jesus promises something, then it is His will. The Lord's presence in His supper isn't hit or miss. He has promised to be there, and He always keeps His promises. Even when our eyes are closed (but we pray they'd be open more and more!).

So, when the pastor gets up at the table to pray, don't be tempted to wonder whether he'll pray well enough to bring down the presence of the Lord. That's not what's going on at all. He's just praying and asking according to Christ's will, as He's revealed it to us in His promise. And so the pastor knows, and we know, that we will have the very thing we ask for. He can pray a prayer like this one from a breaking of bread in Ghana, full of faith that the Lord will indeed answer:

> *Heavenly Father, we thank You for this opportunity to break bread with You. We pray that this bread, made by men, would be cleansed and sanctified and made holy, and that it would become Christ's body indeed. As we partake of this one, we are partaking of His body, in the name of Jesus. Amen.*
>
> *Father, this wine was made by men, but we lift it up before You. Cleanse it and wash it in Christ's blood, and make it holy; and that it would be His blood indeed. As we partake of this wine, we are partaking of Christ's*

blood, and the power in the blood will have effect in our life, in the name of Jesus. Amen.[4]

Yes, there is wonder-working power in prayer—not because our prayers are so wonderful that they work wonders, but because the One to whom we pray is the wonderful and wonder-working Father who delights to hear, and answer, our prayers.

WONDER-WORKING BLESSING

In a social media age, it seems that "hashtag blessed" has often become a brag rather than a true recognition of the wondrous things the Lord has done. But in the Bible, blessing is much, much more than a nice holiday, a good meal, some sunshine or a tolerable day at work. True blessing, in the Bible, doesn't come from circumstances or the work of our hands—true blessing comes only from our Triune God. "The God and Father of our Lord Jesus Christ . . . has blessed us with every spiritual blessing in the heavenly places in Christ" (Ephesians 1:3). When we are saved, God raises us up from death to life by His Holy Spirit, who joins us to Jesus, in whom we are blessed. God's blessing by the Spirit in the Son is life for the dead, forgiveness for the guilty, cleansing for sinners, freedom for captives, hope for the hopeless, joy for mourners, a family for orphans, love for the loveless and beauty for ashes. It's not just one of those; true blessing in Christ is all of that and more. It's to be clothed with Christ for righteousness and anointed with Christ's anointing. It's to know Jesus as closest Friend, Brother and Bridegroom of our hearts. It's to have confidence to "come boldly to the throne of grace, that we may obtain mercy and find grace to help in time of need" (Hebrews 4:16), knowing that "my God shall supply all your need according to His riches in glory by Christ Jesus" (Philippians 4:19). It's to know the Lord as our rock, our shield, our strong tower and our exceedingly great reward.

All of this is ours in Christ, for we have been blessed with every spiritual blessing in Him. We're not gathering up blessings one at a time. No. Joined to Jesus, we are blessed in Him. He has given us Himself, and all that's His is now ours.

But it's ours *in Him*. Our blessings aren't independent of Jesus. If we wander from Him, we're wandering from the blessing. For Jesus isn't just the way in. He is always the way, the only way. So, we're blessed through our union with Christ, and as we grow in communion with Christ, we know more and more of the enjoyment of the blessings that are ours in Him.[5]

When Jesus left His disciples on the Mount of Olives and ascended to the Father's right hand, He was in the middle of blessing them. "He led them out as far as Bethany, and He lifted up His hands and blessed them. Now it came to pass, while He blessed them, that He was parted from them and carried up into heaven" (Luke 24:50–51). Christ's hands were still raised in blessing as He rose, and He has never lowered them. Jesus is still blessing His people from heaven's throne. And part of that blessing is the promise of His presence with us. Just before He ascended, He said, "Lo, I am with you always, even to the end of the age" (Matthew 28:20). The ascension wasn't an end to the blessing, nor was it an end to Christ's presence with us—no! The ascended Savior still blesses His people with His presence. We are His, and He is ours. And it's not a long-distance relationship. He comes to us by His Spirit, He comes to us in His Word and He comes to us in bread and wine at His table. The glorified and ascended Lord still blesses us with His presence in powerful ways.

When He speaks His blessing, powerful things happen, very powerful things. Things like feeding five thousand men, besides women and children, with only five loaves and two fish (see Matthew 14:17–21). That's how Jesus fed the multitude: by speaking His blessing! Out there in a "deserted place" (14:13) on the other side of the lake (just like He would do a year later in the Upper Room at the Last Supper), Jesus "took the five loaves and the two fish, and looking up to heaven, He blessed and broke and gave the loaves to the disciples" (Matthew 14:19). And the tiny amount of bread and fish became, through Christ's blessing, far more than enough to feed the vast crowds. So much so that "they took up twelve baskets full of the fragments that remained" (Matthew 14:20). When Jesus speaks His word of blessing, it works wonders.

He still speaks His wonder-working blessing over broken bread. He also speaks it over poured-out wine. And when He speaks His blessing, He gives far beyond what seems possible. "The cup of blessing which we bless, is it not the communion of the blood of Christ? The bread which we break, is it not the communion of the body of Christ?" (1 Corinthians 10:16). Jesus fed a hungry multitude with miraculous quantities of bread and fish. Now at our Communion tables, Jesus feeds a hungry multitude with the miraculous communion of His body and blood—only through His wonder-working word of blessing.

WONDER-WORKING WORD

It shouldn't surprise us that Christ's word of blessing can work such wonders. Throughout the Bible, the Lord is constantly working wonders by His Word, right from the very first page, where God speaks the light—and then all creation—into being by His Word, to the very last book, where the Lord Jesus works His powerful judgment by the sword from His mouth (see Revelation 1:16; 19:15, 21). We see it again and again throughout Christ's earthly ministry as well. Let's take a look in John's gospel.

John points us to seven signs that Jesus performed, demonstrating that He is indeed the Lord. These signs demonstrate His glorious and gracious divine power, and each of them were accomplished by speaking His Word.

Jesus performed the first of His signs at a wedding in Cana of Galilee when He turned water into wine. Right from the beginning of His signs, Jesus "manifested His glory" (John 2:11) using wine! How did He turn water into wine? He simply spoke. His mother told the servants, "Whatever He says to you, do it" (John 2:5), just like Jesus would tell the apostles to "do this" at the Last Supper (Luke 22:19; 1 Corinthians 11:24–25). In both cases, their doing could only be done in connection with Jesus' speaking. Servants often filled waterpots. The miraculous power wasn't in what they did, but in what Jesus spoke.

"Jesus said to them, 'Fill the waterpots with water.' And they filled them up to the brim. And He said to them, 'Draw some out now, and take it to the master of the feast.' And they took it" (John 2:7–8). His word transformed what they did, so that when they took what they drew out to the master of the feast, it wasn't the water that they had put in. Merely by His word, Jesus transformed water into wine. Not just any wine, the best wine (John 2:10). And not just enough wine to get by, but 750 bottles of the choicest of wines![6] By His Word,

Jesus works wonders beyond what is needed. By His Word, Jesus did far beyond what anyone could ask or imagine, and in that way He "manifested His glory" (verse 11).

A while later, Jesus came back to Cana of Galilee and performed another sign by His word. A nobleman came to Jesus and "implored Him to come down and heal his son, for he was at the point of death" (John 4:47). But Jesus did not go down with the nobleman. Instead, He simply spoke His word. "Go your way; your son lives" (John 4:50). And at that exact moment, the man's son was healed (see John 4:53). Even at a great distance, the Lord works wonders—life-giving wonders—by His wonder-working word.

When Jesus went up to Jerusalem, He met a man by the pool of Bethesda who had been waiting for an angel to come and stir up the waters so that he could be healed. But Jesus didn't need to send an angel. He didn't even need to send the man into the pool. Instead, Jesus simply spoke: "Rise, take up your bed and walk" (John 5:8). And the man did! For "immediately the man was made well" (verse 9). Thirty-eight years of infirmity were overcome when Jesus spoke His wonder-working word.

The next sign, we've already seen, when Jesus spoke a blessing, and fed the five thousand (from John 6:11). That night, He performed another when He walked on the waves of the sea. Only because Jesus is God could He walk on the waves (Job 9:8). Yet, in the midst of the wonder of the walking on the water, Jesus also spoke His word. The disciples had seen Him (despite the darkness of being out in the middle of the sea), and they were afraid. Jesus said to them, "It is I; do not be afraid" (John 6:20), and His Word had two results, one natural, and one supernatural. They welcome Him into the boat, and "immediately the boat was at the land where they were going" (verse 21). Christ's wonder-working word was more than able to overcome the limitations of geography.

When Jesus met a man born blind, He combined His word with something physical to give him sight. "He spat on the ground and made clay with the saliva; and He anointed the eyes of the blind man with the clay. And He said to him, 'Go, wash in the pool of Siloam'" (John 9:6–7). The man took Jesus at His word and "went and washed, and came back seeing" (verse 7). Mud can't open the eyes of the blind. But mud joined to Jesus' word has Jesus' power at work. (Just like when water or bread and wine are joined to Jesus' word in baptism and the Lord's Supper!) Christ's power was at work through His mud-covered word, and believing, the blind man received its wonder-working benefit.

Christ's word doesn't only heal and multiply. His wonder-working word gives life to the dead. That's exactly what happened when He spoke to Lazarus, who had been dead and buried for four days. Where Martha—who loved her brother, Lazarus, and trusted Jesus, confessing Him as "the Christ, the Son of God" (John 11:27)—could only foresee "a stench" (verse 39), Jesus spoke life. "Lazarus, come forth!" (verse 43). And Lazarus did. Even the power of death is no match for the power of Christ's wonder-working, life-giving word.

This is the same life-giving word that is spoken week after week, day after day, by Christ's servants over bread and wine at His table. The Word that spoke creation into being, that turned water into wine, that multiplied the loaves, that healed and opened blind eyes, that overcame the physical limits of geography, that raised the dead to life, is the Word spoken at the supper. When Christ's words are spoken at the table, we're not simply hearing someone tell us what was spoken in the Upper Room two thousand years ago. Christ is speaking through His servants, saying to us once again, "This is My body . . . this is My blood." He joins bread and wine to His word to meet us in a wonderful, life-transforming way.

All over the world, in every language, Jesus is speaking His word at His table. He speaks the wonderful Good News that this is His body, given for us and this is His blood, shed for us for the forgiveness of sin. And He wraps up that Good News in bread and wine to feed us and fill us with Himself.

Without Christ's words, bread and wine in church are just a snack. But, set apart by prayer and blessed with Jesus' wonder-working words of institution, this bread and wine are filled, not just with wonder-working power, but with the presence of the wonder-working Savior Himself.

7

Jesus, Our Manna

THE LORD CAN PROVIDE miraculous food. We know He can. He sent ravens to feed Elijah with "bread and meat in the morning, and bread and meat in the evening" at the Brook Cherith (1 Kings 17:6), and then miraculously multiplied the widow of Zarephath's last handful of flour and drop of oil to feed her and her son and the prophet through the rest of the famine (see 1 Kings 17:8–16). He used the prophet Elisha to multiply the oil in one jar to fill a multitude of jars (see 2 Kings 4:1–7), to heal a poisonous, death-producing spring and turn it into life-giving water (see 2 Kings 2:19–22) and to multiply the barley bread to feed a hundred men (see 2 Kings 4:42–44). He Himself multiplied fish and loaves to feed the four thousand and the five thousand, and provided miraculous catches of fish (see Luke 5:1–11; John 21:4–8). He supplied miraculous wine at the wedding in Cana when there was none (see John 2:1–11). And back before any of those things, He sent quail and manna to feed the children of Israel in the wilderness, and He gave them water from the rock to drink (see Exodus 16–17). Providing miraculous food and drink is not too difficult for the Lord of heaven and earth.

HEAVENLY BREAD

The manna in the wilderness was different from every other supply of miraculous food. It wasn't a miracle of multiplication, nor was something else turned into bread. But this was, quite literally, bread from heaven. Psalm 78 tells us that the Lord:

> Had commanded the clouds above, and opened the doors of heaven, had rained down manna on them to eat, and given them of the bread of heaven. Men ate angels' food; He sent them food to the full.
>
> Psalm 78:23–25

The Lord rained this food down from heaven. The manna is so heavenly that it can be called "angels' food." This is truly miraculous bread.

The Lord underscored the miraculous nature of the manna by commanding them to keep a memorial. An omersworth of manna was put in a pot, and the pot was placed in the presence of the Lord in the Ark of the Covenant, along with Aaron's rod that budded and the two stone tablets of the Ten Commandments (see Exodus 16:32–34; Hebrews 9:4). Neither of those things was ordinary. Aaron's rod was a piece of wood cut from a tree. There was no life in it, yet the Lord worked a miracle so that it "sprouted and put forth buds, had produced blossoms and yielded ripe almonds" to show that He had chosen Aaron (Numbers 17:8). The two stone tablets contained the very heart of God's covenant with His people, in words which the Lord Himself had written (see Exodus 34:1, 28; Deuteronomy 10:2, 4).

The Ark held God's own words, something God had raised from the dead to new life, and the bread God had rained down from heaven. These three things were miraculous, and they belonged there in the Holy of Holies, the most holy place in the Tabernacle, under the Mercy Seat with its atoning blood.

This holy, glorious, miraculous bread that both fed God's people and dwelt in God's presence also brought a foretaste of the fulfillment of God's promise for the future. The manna tasted "like wafers made with honey" (Exodus 16:31). And honey was the promised taste of the Promised Land (see Exodus 3:8). This heavenly bread was a foretaste and a pledge of the truth of God's promise. And they ate it until the promise came, for "the manna ceased on the day after they had eaten the produce of the [Promised] land" (Joshua 5:12). There was no bread more glorious, more miraculous, more heavenly or more powerful a pledge of the Lord's goodness in the history of His people than the manna.

THE BREAD OF HEAVEN

Yet Jesus said, "Your fathers ate the manna in the wilderness, and are dead. This is the bread which comes down from heaven, that one may eat of it and not die" (John 6:49–50). Jesus was claiming to have better bread than the bread of angels. Better bread than the bread that had sustained the children of Israel for forty years in the wilderness. Better bread than the bread that sat in the Ark of God's presence alongside God's own handwriting. Better bread than the bread that gave a foretaste of the abundance of God's promised future life. "Most assuredly," Jesus said to them, "Moses did not give you the bread from heaven, but My Father gives you the true bread from heaven. For the bread of God is He who comes down from heaven and gives life to the world" (John 6:32–33). There is a much better Bread than the manna. The manna sustained physical life, but there is a Bread that comes down from heaven and gives true life, full life, spiritual life. And Jesus tells us exactly where to find this Bread: "I am the bread of life. He who comes to Me shall never hunger, and he who believes in Me shall never thirst" (John 6:35). Manna is great and glorious, but it doesn't even begin to compare to Jesus, the true Bread of heaven.

And yet, Jesus uses a discussion of manna to frame His teaching on the Bread of Life. He could have jumped straight from the miracle He'd just performed the day before, feeding the five thousand, to speak of bread. Or He could have mentioned the Passover Lamb to speak about food connected with God's salvation. But He didn't. He chose the manna. For the manna shared some things in common with the true Bread of Heaven that those other foods didn't. The bread that fed the five thousand was miraculous, but it was still merely earthly bread. The Passover lamb was sacrificed, and God delivered those who fed upon it and sheltered under its blood, but it was still merely an earthly lamb. The manna, however, wasn't earthly. The manna was supernatural, heavenly bread. The manna was bread that was at home in the holiest place in the glory of God's presence in the Holy of

Holies. This bread was different from any other. And so is the true Bread of Heaven.

But most of the people who heard Jesus couldn't see how this Bread of Heaven was supernatural at all. Instead, they grumbled and said, "Is not this Jesus, the son of Joseph, whose father and mother we know? How is it then that He says, 'I have come down from heaven'?" (John 6:42). They could only see a natural man, with a human family. But what they couldn't see was that this truly human man who stood before them was also God the Son. They could see the humanity of Christ, but they missed the reality of the incarnate God. (Just as we can be tempted to see only the earthly elements of bread and wine without discerning the supernatural presence of the Lord's body and blood in the supper.)

Jesus answers their grumbling by speaking even more strongly of the power of this greater-than-manna Bread of Heaven. First, He declares the truth of His deity. He is the One who saves, for the Father draws people to Him for salvation. He is the One who will raise the dead on the last day (see John 6:44). Those who truly hear the Father come to Jesus (see John 6:45). And only Jesus has seen the Father (see John 6:46). Then, Jesus continues:

> Most assuredly, I say to you, he who believes in Me has everlasting life. I am the bread of life. Your fathers ate the manna in the wilderness, and are dead. This is the bread which comes down from heaven, that one may eat of it and not die. I am the living bread which came down from heaven. If anyone eats of this bread, he will live forever; and the bread that I shall give is My flesh, which I shall give for the life of the world.
>
> John 6:47–51

The fathers ate the manna in the wilderness and died, but we can eat the Bread of Life and live. And eating the Bread of Life combines two things: believing in Jesus and receiving His flesh. The last isn't minor. Immediately Jesus' hearers "quarreled among themselves, saying, 'How can this Man give us His flesh to eat?'" (John 6:52). They had heard exactly what Jesus was saying. Jesus doesn't rush in to stop the quarrel by telling them they've misunderstood—no! He breaks in to make it even more explicit, saying, "Most assuredly, I say to you, unless you eat the flesh of the Son of Man and drink His blood, you have no life in you" (John 6:53).

JOHN'S HOLY OF HOLIES

John doesn't give us an account of the Last Supper. He didn't need to. Not only had Matthew, Mark, Luke and Paul already written accounts, but even before they had put pen to paper, every church had been celebrating the supper by repeating Christ's words and actions at the very least every Lord's Day (but often much more frequently than that). Long before the Church had the New Testament in written form, it had the New Covenant in Christ's blood. "Before there was a Bible to hold us together, there was our Lord's Supper. The Church of Jesus Christ existed for decades without New Testament Scriptures, but we did not exist for a single week without the New Testament of Jesus' Holy Supper."[1] John and all the churches he was writing for knew the Lord's Supper by heart. He didn't need to repeat it.

But that doesn't mean John doesn't teach us anything about the breaking of bread. The main reason John leaves out the institution of the sacrament in the Upper Room is, in the words of Adolph Saphir, "because throughout John, more than any other part of the New Testament, the spiritual meaning of the Lord's Supper is dwelt upon."[2] And Jesus' reply to this quarrel in chapter 6 about how He could give His flesh to eat is the very holy of holies of John's teaching on the supper. Instead of giving us his own words about the supper, John gives us Jesus' own words about eating His flesh and drinking His blood.

> Whoever eats My flesh and drinks My blood has eternal life, and I will raise him up at the last day. For My flesh is food indeed, and My blood is drink indeed. He who eats My flesh and drinks My blood abides in Me, and I in him. As the living Father sent Me, and I live because of the Father, so he who feeds on Me will live because of Me. This is the bread which came down from heaven—not as your fathers ate the manna, and are dead. He who eats this bread will live forever.
>
> John 6:54–58

The people have been quarreling about the merest mention of eating Christ's flesh. And Jesus does not explain it away. Instead, just in case anyone got confused, He starts using a different word for "eat." Up to verse 54, He'd used the normal word for "eat," but then He switches to a much more physical word—a cruder word that has the idea of chewing, or gnawing, or eating in a noisy way. In no way does Jesus weaken His language about eating His flesh; He strengthens it.

And to that He adds something even more scandalous: He starts talking about drinking His blood. In the Old Testament, drinking blood was strictly forbidden. The Lord had said that "whatever man of the house of Israel, or of the strangers who dwell among you, who eats any blood, I will set My face against that person who eats blood, and will cut him off from among his people. . . . You shall not eat the blood of any flesh, for the life of all flesh is its blood. Whoever eats it shall be cut off" (Leviticus 17:10, 14). Blood was only to be used "upon the altar to make atonement" (Leviticus 17:11), never for drinking. And yet Jesus says that unless we drink His blood, we have no life is us. In the Old Testament Law, drinking blood meant being cut off from the Lord and His people—a living death. But in this New Testament that Jesus has established in His blood, whoever drinks His blood has eternal life and will be raised up by Christ to resurrection life on the last day. Those who ate the manna—the bread that fell from heaven itself—died, but those who drink Christ's blood will live.

This is mind-blowing. The crowd couldn't cope. Even many of Jesus' disciples couldn't handle it and abandoned Him from that point on (see John 6:66). Yet, although they found it "a hard saying" (verse 60), the Twelve stayed and clung to Jesus. Why? The words may have been hard, but they recognized that these are "the words of eternal life" (verse 68).

Jesus doesn't just say a hard thing; He gives a precious promise. He promises life-giving power through His body and blood. Those who eat His flesh and drink His blood have eternal life and will be raised from the dead to glorious resurrection life. But this isn't a magic promise. Jesus does not say "do this" and you'll have life—no! He says, "Eat My flesh and drink My blood, and you'll have Me—the One who is the Way, the Truth, and the Life—with all My life-giving and death-defeating power living in you." Whoever eats Christ's flesh and drinks His blood abides in Christ and Christ abides in them. Bread and wine have no life-giving power in themselves; only Jesus has. And the promise of the power of the Lord's Supper lies in the presence of Jesus Himself.

BUT HOW?

Jesus doesn't give an answer to the crowd about how He could give His flesh to eat. He holds out the promise of life through His body and blood; He holds out Himself as the only way to eternal life. And they walk away.

But afterward, when Jesus saw the confusion of His disciples, He explained more:

> When Jesus knew in Himself that His disciples complained about this, He said to them, "Does this offend you? What then if you should see the Son of Man ascend where He was before? It is the Spirit who gives life; the flesh profits nothing. The words that I speak to you are spirit, and they are life. . . ." But Simon Peter answered Him, "Lord, to whom shall we go? You have the words of eternal life. Also we have come to believe and know that You are the Christ, the Son of the living God."
>
> John 6:61–63, 68–69

Again, Jesus doesn't try to soften His words or explain them away. There are other times when the disciples misunderstood what He was saying and He set them straight. When He told them to "beware of the leaven of the Pharisees and the leaven of Herod" (Mark 8:15), the disciples misunderstood and "reasoned among themselves, saying, 'It is because we have no bread'" (verse 16). But Jesus made clear that they had misunderstood what He was telling them: "Why do you reason because you have no bread? Do you not yet perceive nor understand?" (verse 17).

But in John 6, when people think Jesus is talking about actually eating His flesh and drinking His blood, He doesn't tell them they've misunderstood. He doesn't correct what they think they've heard.

Instead of giving them a different meaning, He speaks to them about how it could be possible to eat His flesh and drink His blood. Merely on earth, it wouldn't be possible—but the answer isn't an earthly one; it's a heavenly one. Jesus is talking about eating the flesh and drinking the blood of the glorified, risen, and ascended God-Man.

His reply points them to three things. The first is His ascension into heaven. Jesus asks, "What then if you should see the Son of Man ascend where He was before?" (John 6:62). When He says that, He isn't only speaking about the fact of the ascension, but the identity of the One who ascends. The place He's ascending to isn't a new location; He's already been there. So His words point us to a *before*. Before He descended. Before He came into this world. Before He took on our flesh and blood. And John tells us later in his gospel exactly what was before all that, when Jesus prays, "Now, O Father, glorify Me together with Yourself, with the glory which I had with You before the world was" (John 17:5).

Jesus is returning to the glory He had with the Father before the world was. In fact, as God, He has never departed from that glory. He was always the One "who came down from heaven, that is, the Son of Man who is in heaven" (John 3:13). But now, as the God-Man, He has ascended to the Father's right hand in glory. And as the God-Man, He is now seated on the throne of heaven, and His human nature shares in His divine glory.

Jesus is telling His disciples—and telling us—that it's as the God-Man raised in the glory of the Father that He calls us to eat His flesh and drink His blood. He can give His body and blood for us to eat and drink because He isn't just a man. He is the God-Man. By His divine power, He can give His people on earth His flesh to eat and His blood to drink. By His divine power, He can feed us with His body and blood in the supper.

The second thing Jesus' reply points to is the nature of His flesh. He says, "It is the Spirit who gives life; the flesh profits nothing" (John 6:63). Now, we need to be careful here. This is one of the most misinterpreted verses in the Bible. For centuries, people have been tearing it out of context to try to make it say the opposite of what Jesus is saying here. Jesus has just been telling us a lot about the life-giving power of His flesh. But now He says the flesh is of no avail. What's going on?

Well, flesh *by itself* is of no avail. Mere human flesh has no life-giving power. All the way back in the fifth century, Cyril of Alexandria explained it like this:

When the nature of flesh is considered alone and in itself, it will clearly not be life-giving. It will in no way give life to anything that exists, but it itself needs the one who can give life. However, when the mystery of [Christ's incarnation] is diligently investigated and you learn who dwells in that flesh, you will be altogether confident. . . . Since it has been united to the life-giving Word, it has risen to the power of the better nature and has become life-giving in its entirety. . . . So even though the nature of the flesh is in itself too weak to be able to give life, nevertheless it will do so because it has the life-giving

Word, and it is full of his entire activity. The body belongs, after all, to him who is life by nature, not to anyone earthly.[3]

By the union of Christ's human nature and His divine nature in one person, His flesh is the flesh of God the Son, in whom "dwells all the fullness of the Godhead bodily" (Colossians 2:9). His flesh is the flesh of the One to whom the Father "has granted . . . life in Himself" (John 5:26). And so His flesh is life-giving flesh.

The third thing Jesus speaks of in His reply in John 6 is the nature of His Word: "The words that I speak to you are spirit, and they are life" (verse 63). Peter and the apostles recognized Jesus' words as "the words of eternal life" (verse 68). Jesus' words are the words of God and are filled with the life of God. And Jesus' words are Spirit-filled words, for the Triune God speaks with one voice. The Father speaks His Word in His Son by His Spirit. Word and Spirit can never be divided, because the Trinity can never be divided.

Now, John's readers would have heard some words of Jesus—words filled with the Spirit and with the life of God— week after week as they came to the Lord's table. They would have heard Jesus' words, "This is My body . . . this is My blood." Just as we hear these words of our Savior week after week as we gather at His table. And these words that we hear every time we come to the table, which may have become so familiar and ordinary to us, are words of eternal life. These words of institution are words that are Spirit and life. Because they are the words of Jesus. Each time we hear them at the table, Jesus is speaking them. We don't just hear an account of something that happened a long time ago when we hear Christ's words at the table. Whoever eats His flesh and drinks His blood has eternal life, not because bread and wine give life, but because that bread and wine are joined to Jesus' life-giving, Spirit-filled words, and by those words joined to His life-giving body and blood. Jesus' word does what He says. He says, "This is My body," and, therefore, it is.

Jesus doesn't explain the exact mechanics behind eating His body and drinking His blood. But He points us to what makes it possible for us. Not because of anything earthly, but because of the heavenly realities of the divine power of the ascended Lord, the unity of the one—true God and true Man—Person of Christ, and the effective power of Jesus' words.

These three heavenly truths don't point to one single explanation of Christ's presence in the supper. My goal here isn't to argue you into one particular view.[4] Instead, these draw us simply to revere and say:

> I do not probe into his power but rather marvel at his benevolence. I do not scrutinize his majesty but rather venerate his kindness. I believe in the presence. I am not concerned with the mode of His presence, although I know it is he most certainly present in the closest and most intimate manner.[5]

We cannot comprehend the fullness of the mystery of His presence, but we can, in faith, hold on to His promise that He is there in His Supper where He gives us His body to eat and His blood to drink, and by that we dwell in Him and He in us.

THE MAIN THING

Throughout history, people have kept coming back to John's Holy of Holies to see afresh the glory of the main thing in the supper. And not just in the early Church or the Reformation. Early Pentecostals came to John 6 to gaze on the wonder of the main thing in the supper too. Reading John 6, they couldn't conclude anything other than "we drink His blood; we eat His flesh,"[6] and thus "the Lord's presence is the main thing."[7] But the presence of the Lord in the supper isn't just something to be gazed upon from a distance. As one of Britain's Pentecostal pioneers put it, "Christ declared if we eat His flesh and drink His blood we shall live. So there must be a participation."[8] We need to partake of His presence. We need to actually eat and drink, and we need to do so with faith. Without faith, we cannot eat Christ's body and drink His blood rightly. Without faith, we cannot receive the benefits of eating Christ's body and drinking His blood. Whoever eats and drinks without faith "eats and drinks in an unworthy manner" and so "eats and drinks judgment to himself, not discerning the Lord's body" (1 Corinthians 11:29). Jesus says, "My flesh is true food, and my blood is true drink" (John 6:55 ESV). So we need to truly eat His body and truly drink His blood at the Lord's table, and we need to eat and drink with faith.

8

I Stand Amazed in the Presence

JESUS IS PRESENT in the breaking of bread. He told us that right from the beginning when He instituted this holy supper in the Upper Room. "This is My body . . . this is My blood," He said. Jesus is present in the supper as our mighty Savior. Jesus is present in the supper to forgive and cleanse. And Jesus is present in the supper to open our eyes to the glory and grace of His presence, in which there is fullness of joy.

Jesus said, "He who eats My flesh and drinks My blood abides in Me, and I in him" (John 6:56). His body and blood are present so that, by them, Jesus Himself will abide in us, and we in Him.

Charles Spurgeon was overjoyed by this truth. Every Sunday, Spurgeon longed to meet with Jesus at His table. Even when he was traveling, he would find some fellow believers and hold a breaking of bread. Why? Because, as he explained it, in the supper

> We enter the holy of holies, and come to the most sacred meeting-place between our souls and God. . . . That He is here we are sure, for here is His flesh, and here is His blood. You see the outward tokens, may you feel the unseen reality; for we believe in His real presence.[1]

At a breaking of bread in Menton on the French Riviera, Spurgeon reminded the gathered believers that

> He calls upon us to eat bread with Him; yea, to partake of Himself, by eating His flesh and drinking His blood. Oh, that we may pass beyond the outward signs into the closest intimacy with Himself![2]

Spurgeon didn't want anyone just to see bread and wine and miss what was really offered at the table. Jesus is present. And He's present to draw us into intimate communion with Himself.

IN YOUR PRESENCE IS FULLNESS OF JOY

Where Jesus is present, fullness of joy is found (see Psalm 16:11). The early Church knew that. You might have been surprised at their joy. After all, Jesus had been taken from them on the clouds. He had ascended out of their sight into heaven. And yet, those earliest years of the Church were full of joy. We see it over and over again in the book of Acts (see 2:41, 46; 5:41; 8:8, 39; 11:23; 12:14; 13:48, 52; 15:3, 31; 16:34; 20:24). But then, those disciples in the early Church knew that things weren't as they might seem. To others it might look like Jesus was gone and they were on their own. But they knew differently. The risen Lord had left them a promise just before He ascended, saying, "Lo, I am with you always, even to the end of the age" (Matthew 28:20). And after He ascended, "They went out and preached everywhere, the Lord working with them and confirming the word through accompanying signs" (Mark 16:20). He made His presence known to them in His Word and by His Holy Spirit. And they knew that He'd promised His presence in a glorious, gracious and powerful way in the breaking of bread. Because they knew that, their breaking of bread was full of joy.

> So continuing daily with one accord in the temple, and break-
> ing bread from house to house, they ate their food with glad-
> ness and simplicity of heart, praising God and having favor
> with all the people. And the Lord added to the church daily
> those who were being saved.
>
> Acts 2:46–47

Every day they met with Jesus in the breaking of bread, and as they ate the holy food of His body and blood, they were filled with gladness. In His presence they found fullness of joy. Their communion with Christ at His table led to continual praising of God. And it led to God working through them to save others and add to the Church. As we rejoice in the presence of Christ at His table, the Lord can work through us to bring others to rejoice in Christ and His salvation too.

We're invited to come and feast on the Lord's presence at His table, knowing that in His "presence is fullness of joy" (Psalm 16:11). Not just a little joy. Fullness of joy. Other things might make us happy. Lesser things might cheer us up. But none of them can give the fullness of joy that's found only in the presence of the Lord. "We are," C. S. Lewis wrote, "half-hearted creatures, fooling about with drink and sex and ambition when infinite joy is offered us, like an ignorant child who wants to go on making mud pies in a slum because he cannot imagine what is meant by an offer of a holiday at the sea. We are far too easily pleased."[3] Too often, like the mud pie–making child, we lose sight of where we'll find true joy. We imagine we'll find it in the things of this world, because that's where everyone else is looking. That's where films, and novels, and television programs, and politicians, and celebrities, and—sadly, all too often—even other Christians send us to look. But our hope is not in our best life now. For if it is, then, in the words of the apostle Paul, "We are of all men the most pitiable" (1 Corinthians 15:19). Our hope is in heaven, "where Christ is, sitting at the right hand of God" (Colossians 3:1). Our hope is in the presence of our crucified, risen, and glorified Savior. And so, if we're to know true joy—full joy—we'll need to "seek those things which are above" and set our minds on them, "not on things on the earth" (Colossians 3:1–2).

We can set our minds on things above as we meditate on God's Word and contemplate the beauty of Jesus. At any—and every—moment, we can seek those things that are above. Yet there is a promised place where those things from above reach us in a special way: when heaven and earth meet in the breaking of bread as Jesus feeds us with His body and blood. At the supper, we don't simply set our minds on Christ's heavenly presence; we encounter Christ's heavenly presence. The presence in which there is fullness of joy.

Where is Jesus now? He is at God's right hand. So when we meet Jesus at His table, we are brought to the right hand of God. And the right hand of God is the exact place where Psalm 16 tells us we'll find fullness of joy and pleasures forevermore.

This joy and pleasure at God's right hand is not found in limited supply. The joy is full, and the pleasure lasts forever. We don't need to use it sparingly. Rather, when we lack joy, we can run freely to the presence of Jesus and receive of the abundant, unlimited supply that comes only from Him. Sometimes when we're lacking in joy, our natural tendency is to avoid the Lord's presence. We stay at a distance by avoiding reading His Word, not meditating on Scripture or spending time with Him in prayer or gathering for worship with the Church. Yet what we most need in those joyless situations is an encounter with the presence of the Lord! So don't avoid meeting with the Lord in prayer, or in His Word, or at His table. Run into His presence—the presence where fullness of joy and lasting pleasures are found. And cry out to Him to experience the reality of His presence as you come to Him in prayer, in His Word and in the breaking of bread.

UNION AND COMMUNION

Before we go any further, let's just clear up something that might cause some confusion. Jesus tells us that whoever "eats My flesh and drinks My blood abides in Me, and I in him"

(John 6:56). This abiding or dwelling in Jesus involves two things: *union* with Christ and *communion* with Christ. Only those who are united to Christ in faith can rightly eat His body and drink His blood. And our union with Christ is strengthened and sustained by feeding on Him in the supper.

Now, that's a bit hard to understand. Union with Christ isn't a process. Either we're united to Him or we're not. When God raises us from death in our sins and transgressions to new life in Christ, He unites us to Christ by the Holy Spirit through faith. So, if you've been born again, you have been united to Christ. We can't be any more united or any less united to Jesus. You either are or you aren't. We're either *in Christ* or we're not.

Yet the Lord sustains and strengthens this union in the supper, as we feed upon Christ's body and blood. Our union with Jesus doesn't ebb and flow, but it does need to be strengthened and sustained. Being united to Christ isn't a step you pass through, like some sort of advance to the next level of a video game. Being united to Christ is an ongoing connection to a living person. And the way that connection to Him is maintained is through faith. Whatever strengthens and builds up our faith in Jesus, strengthens and sustains our union with Him. The supper does that. Or rather, Jesus does that in His supper by feeding us with His body and blood.

Our whole salvation flows from our union with Christ. United to Him, we are blessed "with every spiritual blessing in the heavenly places in Christ" (Ephesians 1:3). So our union with Christ is the only foundation for the whole of our Christian life.

Which brings us to the second part of our abiding in Christ and Christ abiding in us: *communion* with Christ. Communion with Christ isn't the same thing as union with Christ, although it is rooted in it. You can't have true communion with Christ unless you're in union with Christ. And, unlike our union, our communion can ebb and flow. Communion is a relationship, not a fixed state.

So, what does communion actually mean? The great Puritan pastor and theologian John Owen wrote a wonderful book to try to explain the nature of the communion believers have with the Triune God. He describes it as "the mutual sharing of those good things which delight all those in that fellowship. . . . Our communion with God lies in his giving himself to us and our giving ourselves and all that he requires to him."[4] Our union with Christ depends entirely on what God has done *for* us in Jesus and *in* us by the Holy Spirit. But our communion with Christ is a two-way relationship. Communion is sharing a good relationship, as Christ abides in us and we abide in Him.

Unlike our union with Christ, our communion with Christ can grow. We grow in our love for Christ and our delight in Him. As Owen puts it, real communion is a life full of "renewed acts of receiving and embracing Christ all our days."[5] And where do we receive and embrace Christ more intimately than in His body and blood in the supper? That's why the supper is a feast, because in it "believers are richly entertained by Christ, having sweet intimacy with Him and great expressions of His love."[6]

During the Nadere Reformatie (the Dutch second Reformation), Wilhelmus à Brakel wrote of this wonderful communion with Christ in the supper as:

none other than a portal of heaven. . . . Heaven opens itself in such a place, and the rays of divine glory and grace descend to that place, filling it with the very presence of God. . . . The Lord Jesus, the Bridegroom, comes in His love. . . . Here is the household of God, and here spiritual friends are gathered together for a moment in order to delight themselves in the presence of . . . Jesus, their beloved Bridegroom.[7]

This is just how Pentecostals experienced the breaking of bread a few hundred years later too. In their Lord's Suppers, "He whose presence makes heaven itself what it is, became a reality in our midst."[8] The breaking of bread is heaven on earth.

"To be joyful in God is heaven," wrote à Brakel.[9] And here below, "all joy and happiness consist in having communion with Him."[10] Communion with Christ is heaven on earth. And at the table that's what's offered to us: a foretaste of the unending, heavenly joy found only in communion with Jesus.

Our words can't even describe the bliss of this joy in Jesus. Throughout the history of the Church, people have tried to describe it a bit, but mostly given up as they've been caught up in the glory. This communion is "sweetness and overflowing delight" and "strong and loving comfort."[11] It's "a foretaste of the consummation when I shall say: 'And lo, O Lord, I am with Thee for all eternity!'"[12] It's to "behold the amazing, infinite, and immutable love of God [and] rejoice with joy unspeakable and full of glory."[13]

A Welsh Pentecostal hymn expressed the communion with Christ we enjoy in the supper like this:

> The earth's best glories
> And the world's highest esteem,
> Fade away into nothingness,
> In enjoying Your countenance;

Your smiles are the sun of the heavens,
Eternal summer is Your face,
And delight for endless ages
In enjoying Your feast of love.[14]

Another Welsh Pentecostal (one who often sat at the same Lord's table as the writer of the hymn) described this enjoying the smile of Christ in communion like what happened to Peter, James and John on the Mount of Transfiguration:

> The experience of the three disciples has been the privilege of some of us also. We, too, have ascended the Mount with Him . . . and men have been lost sight of in the sublimity of His Presence . . . although it behooves us to hold the Lord's counsel with reverence, for the Lord charges His disciples . . . saying, "Tell the Vision to no man!"[15]

The inexpressible glories of communion with Christ are too wonderful to tell. But we don't need to be able to describe them. We're invited to do something much better. We're invited to come to Jesus at the table and "taste and see that the LORD is good" (Psalm 34:8).

THE FEAST OF LOVE

What we can say about our communion with Christ in the supper is that it is a feast of love. So it shouldn't surprise us that all through history, Christians have kept going back to the Song of Solomon to find the best expressions of what this communion is really like. Because the Song of Solomon is a song of the love between a Bride and her glorious, royal

Bridegroom, who comes "out of the wilderness like pillars of smoke, perfumed with myrrh and frankincense" (Song of Solomon 3:6). And who is the King who came out of the wilderness like a pillar of smoke? It's Jesus, who "saved the people out of the land of Egypt" (Jude 5) and led them through the wilderness in a pillar of cloud by day and a pillar of fire by night. Who is the King perfumed with myrrh and frankincense? It's Jesus, who received frankincense and myrrh from the wise men as an infant and whose body was anointed with myrrh for burial (see John 19:39–40). Jesus is the true glorious royal Bridegroom and His Church is His Bride. The Song of Solomon is pointing us to the great love of Christ for us, His Church.

In the second chapter, we read about love and delight in feasting at the banqueting table. It's the Bride who is speaking here, describing the feast of love her Bridegroom provides.

> Like an apple tree among the trees of the woods, so is my beloved among the sons. I sat down in his shade with great delight, and his fruit was sweet to my taste. He brought me to the banqueting house, and his banner over me was love. Sustain me with cakes of raisins, refresh me with apples, for I am lovesick. His left hand is under my head, and his right hand embraces me.
>
> Song of Solomon 2:3–6

At this feast of love at the Bridegroom's banqueting table, there is refreshing in His presence. Like an apple tree in the heat of the summer, He is our shelter, our refuge and our shade (see Psalms 143:9; 46:7; 121:5). He protects us from the ravages of the desert heat and provides for us a place of peace and security. But not only does He protect and provide, He also feeds His Bride with fruit that is sweet to taste. As we shelter in the shadow of our Savior, He feeds us with His sweetness in His supper. And as we abide in Him, the sweet fruit with which He feeds us will go on to produce much fruit in us (see John 15:4–5, 8).

As the Bridegroom meets His Bride at His banqueting table in His house of wine,[16] His banner over us is love. Our heavenly Bridegroom displays His love and affection toward us at His table of wine, as the wonders of His death are proclaimed and we are fed with His body and blood. For "in this is love, not that we loved God, but that He loved us and sent His Son to be the propitiation for our sins" (1 John 4:10). Propitiation is a sacrifice that takes the wrath of God. As Jesus' death in our place (paying the penalty for our sins) is proclaimed in the supper, we see the true love of God in Christ displayed. This bread and wine of the supper are the tokens of the great love of the Triune God for us. The breaking of bread makes God's love to us visible. "We love Him because He first loved us" (1 John 4:19). He shows us that love, a love that draws out our love in return, each time we celebrate the supper.

At His banqueting table, there is a rich abundance of delightful food. This isn't an ad-hoc picnic table with some plain food to see us on our way. No, it's a table of rich, sweet provisions. It's an abundant feast to enjoy, that's refreshing as well as sustaining. And it's a meal that overwhelms us with the incredible love of our Bridegroom, leaving us "lovesick" (Song of Solomon 2:5) and longing for more and more of His loving presence.

That loving presence is what He delights to give us at His table of wine. "His left hand is under my head, and his right hand embraces me" (2:6). At His table, the Lord Jesus, our glorious, heavenly Bridegroom, holds us in His love. We don't only find blessings from Christ in His supper, we find His loving presence. And the presence of Jesus is never a disinterested presence. Christ delights in His people, and so at His table we find His loving embrace. This isn't just a table of glory; it's a table of intimacy. For it's the table of Christ's deep love for us.

GAZING AT THE GLORY

Throughout the centuries, as Christ's people have beheld Him in His glory in the supper, they have experienced the joy of His deep love. In eating His flesh and drinking His blood, they've found intimate communion with the One who loved them and gave Himself for them. Most have probably kept that to themselves and Jesus. But we have a lot of testimonies that have been written down over the years too.

A thousand years ago, with some reticence, Symeon wrote of his experience of the presence of the Lord in the supper. (He followed the example of the apostle Paul when he wrote of his unspeakable experience in 2 Corinthians 12:2–4 by saying, "I know a man in Christ. . . .") Symeon described this communion as "beholding what I had never beheld before" and as astonishing light.[17] Symeon (who would later get the title "the New Theologian") experienced this astonishing, indescribable communion every time he went to the Lord's table. Others through the centuries have, at times, seen this shining light of the Lord's presence in the supper. In the ninth century, Ignatius of Constantinople once saw it, and so did the congregation gathered at the Lord's table with him. Hildegard of Bingen saw it at one celebration of the supper in the twelfth century. Some have had glimpses of this light in more recent years too.

Sometime after the Reformation, Isaac Ambrose tells us about a godly woman who came to the Lord's supper full of despair. Her despair was taken away when she ate and drank at the Lord's table. She "was filled with such unspeakable joys, that she knew not how she got home; which soul-ravishing joys continued for a fortnight after, and filled her mouth with songs of praise, so that she could neither sleep nor eat, more than she forced herself to do out of conscience of duty."[18]

Isaac Ambrose himself wrote in his diary of his experience of the comfortable presence of Christ in the supper, as well as "sweet visits" and "spiritual refreshing." At one Communion in 1648, he described how he "felt many sweet impressions of God's Spirit in his heart, sometimes melting, and sometimes cheering his soul" in the supper.[19]

On Whitsunday (the Day of Pentecost) in 1735, a man named Howell Harris went to a Communion service in his parish church in Wales. He'd been reading a book that had lifted his eyes to see the reality of the powerful grace of Jesus in the supper.[20] In his diary, Harris described what happened that day: "At the Table, Christ bleeding on the cross was kept before my eyes constantly; and strength was given me to believe that I was receiving pardon on account of the blood. I lost my burden: I went home leaping for joy. . . . Oh blessed day!"[21]

Around the same time, in another part of Wales, Daniel Rowland was the minister of Llangeitho in Cardiganshire. Not only he, but many in his congregation, suddenly began to encounter the reality of the presence of the Lord as they celebrated the supper. "There is such power as I have never felt before, given me in preaching and administering the Lord's Supper. The Lord comes down among us in such a manner as words can give no idea of."[22] At first, Daniel tried to calm the reaction of the people to the presence of the Lord. But he had to give up. "Such is the light, view, and power God gives very many in the [Supper], that they cannot possibly help crying out, praising and adoring Jesus, being quite swallowed up in God; and thus I was obliged to leave my whole congregation, being many hundreds, in a flame . . . this is our condition generally every Sabbath."[23] This wasn't a one-off. This was every Lord's Day. And it wasn't one or two people. It was the whole congregation aflame through the light and power of Christ in the supper. In fact, a huge revival broke out at a Communion service in Daniel Rowland's church that engulfed the whole of Wales.

In 1742 a revival broke out in a town in Scotland called Cambuslang. Later, the minister gathered together as many testimonies as he could of what the Lord did in the lives of people who had been part of the revival. There are too many to tell them all, but I'll give you a few examples. Kathleen Stuart was a nineteen-year-old seamstress from Glasgow who was "filled with love to God and allowed much communion with Him, and felt inexpressible sweetness" at the supper. Coming forward to the Lord's table, she "could scarcely walk; I was swallowed up in love and inflamed affections to the Redeemer, and melted down in sorrow for my sins." But then, as she ate and drank:

> I was allowed near access to God by faith. . . . When the sacramental bread came to my hand, that word came with great

power to my heart, "This is My body broken for you," and when I had taken the cup into my hand, that word was struck into my mind with great power, "This is My blood shed for you." . . . I was astonished at the great love of God in Christ to me. . . . At that sacramental occasion, my heart was more enlarged than ever.[24]

Rebecca Dykes, a teenager, said that as she was eating and drinking at the supper, she was filled with "such a love to Christ that I thought I could have died for Him," and this love made her "long after conformity to Him" when she went from the table. At the next Communion, she was filled with "love and joy I cannot express."[25]

James Tenant, a young man in his early twenties, had "such a manifestation of His love at His table."[26] Another man around the same age, R. Barclay, said:

I came to the Lord's Table with holy fear and reverence . . . at that instant I felt as in a trance, and saw divine justice stretching out its hand to take hold of me, and Christ . . . stepping in betwixt justice and me, showing His wounds and what He had suffered for me in satisfying justice, and saying I have satisfied for his sins; upon which the hand of justice could not touch me. . . . Recovering out of that trance, I felt my soul filled with great joy and comfort.[27]

Mr. Barclay wasn't the only person to have a vision at the breaking of bread. When Catherine Cameron had eaten and drunk of the sacrament, she "was led . . . to the gate of heaven, and made to behold and see a crown of glory there laid up for me. I got the assurance and persuasion of my eternal happiness with Christ."[28] But even before that, Catherine had been overwhelmed with the glory of communion with Jesus in the supper. "On Sabbath morning, coming within view of the Communion table, my heart was . . . melted down within me at the thought of Christ's sufferings, and filled with joy that I would be allowed to sit down at my Master's table here."[29] When she sat down at the table, her heart was further melted, and then, as she drank from the cup, "He said to me, 'My blood is sufficient to wash away all thy sins.' As I was coming away from the table, these words came in, 'Be of good cheer, thy sins are forgiven thee.'"[30]

At that Communion service, between thirty and fifty thousand people had gathered, of whom three thousand had been admitted to the Lord's table, so it took all day to serve Communion to those who were hungry to feed on Christ.[31] (They didn't believe in rushing the Communion in those days.) The breaking of bread began at half past eight in the morning, and the last people were served at sunset. Then there was a sermon that went on until 10 p.m. Catherine was one of the first people to receive Communion, so for the rest of the day, she:

> sat down near the tables and sang psalms with the congregation with much joy, and every now and then I behooved to rise and take another view of my Lord's Table, and felt my heart burn within me with love to Christ and to His ministers and to the communicants and people. I cannot express the joy with which I was filled while the tables were serving. I could not endure to look down to the earth, but looked up mostly to heaven, and thought I heard Christ speaking to me from thence, and saying, "Arise, My love,

my fair one, and come away." I saw Him as it were reaching down His hand and drawing me up to Himself, and at the same time I felt my heart powerfully drawn to Him with the cords of love.[32]

Another young woman, Ann Montgomery, said, "The Lord by His Spirit set home many gracious words (though not uttered by the minister) on my heart, with great power and sweetness, and gave me such manifestations of His love that I had never met with anything like it before."[33]

In 1858, the presence of the Lord was powerfully manifest to everyone who received Communion at a service in a Welsh theological college. As one communicant described it, "We seemed . . . to have arrived at the vestibule of heaven, where we could breathe its pure atmosphere, and join in the song of the redeemed in glory." Those who partook of the supper felt "an influence . . . which we have never experienced in like manner before. . . . It electrified us and caused us to weep with joy." They not only knew by faith that they were communing with Christ, but they felt it powerfully too, as the supper was "filled with the special presence of God."[34]

At another Welsh breaking of bread during the next century, that same special presence of God and entrance into heaven to join in the song of glory were experienced in a profoundly powerful way. At the Apostolic Church's Convention in Penygroes, Carmarthenshire, the congregation packed into the church, filling the floor and the galleries, as they gathered around the Lord's table for the breaking of bread. "And the Divine unction rested upon the congregation, whose fervent prayers, praises and adoration ascended in the Holy Presence. For His atoning Death on the Cross

Jesus was glorified that morning in the sanctity of His People worshipping at His Feet, and we felt ourselves one with the Heavenly throng while singing, 'Holy, holy, holy.'"[35]

The next year, in Hull in the north of England, E. C. W. Boulton described how people experienced the Lord's presence in the supper on Easter Sunday. "How real was the presence of Him at Whose feet we knelt—how our hearts glowed with an unquenchable fire of devotion to the One Who had so freely accomplished our deliverance from the penalty and power of sin by the sacrifice of Himself on Calvary."[36]

At the very beginning of the Pentecostal revival in Europe, at a breaking of bread with people gathered from several different countries in a castle in Germany, the early German Pentecostal leader Jonathan Paul saw the Lord Himself "as the Chalice and the large plate of bread were solemnly passed round after he had reverently used the words of institution and blessing."[37]

On the other side of the Atlantic, A. J. Tomlinson (an early American Pentecostal leader) wrote of seeing Jesus manifest His presence as the bread was broken at the Lord's supper in Cleveland, Tennessee. "As I stood there," he said, "in the presence of God and before the large [congregation] with the broken bread, a piece in each hand, I seemed to get a broader view of the Christ and [His] wonderful scheme of redemption than ever before." So glorious was the Lord's presence that "to describe it would be impossible."[38]

As the Pentecostal missionary Willie Burton put it, "What feasts we have at His table! How He satisfies us! How we love to linger there! How often we go forth from that spiritual feast like giants refreshed!"[39] And that's because Christ's "presence is realized at the Feast which He instituted," for it is there that we "commune with our Lord."[40] In the breaking of bread "we . . . feast on the Lord Jesus, in all His glorious reality."[41]

THE QUESTION OF JOY

I could have ended this chapter with those exciting stories of the joy and glory and inexpressible love of communion with Christ in His supper. Those testimonies encourage me, and I hope they encourage you too. However, I am a real-life pastor, and so I know it's not a good idea to leave you there. I need to go a bit further and answer a very important question. Because you may have never experienced anything like that. And maybe, instead of encouraging you, it's bothering you. Perhaps you're thinking, *Well, I've been eating at the Lord's table every week for years, and I've never experienced any of that!* Maybe you're wondering if there is something wrong with your experience.

First, let me say that we need to be careful with testimonies. These are just a few accounts among billions of the Lord's children celebrating the supper since the Day of Pentecost. The Cambuslang testimonies do have some particularly powerful accounts of communion with Christ at His table, but they're also very valuable in this: They contain accounts from many of the *very same people* telling of other times they went to the Lord's table and didn't feel a thing. The Bible says nothing about our feelings at the Lord's supper. Jesus is there, whether we feel it or not. *Faith* is what's necessary when we come to the breaking of bread, not a particular type of feeling.

And yet, in Christ's presence is fullness of joy. Does that not mean we need to feel something in the supper? A few hundred years ago Guilelmus Saldenus, a pastor in the Netherlands, gave careful thought to this and wrote a little book to help the people in the churches there.[42] Saldenus realized that something is wrong if we "do not seek any spiritual joy in and by means of the Lord's Supper."[43] But he also realized we can so easily be "greatly ensnared by [our] feelings."[44] True joy and exciting, joyful feelings aren't necessarily the same thing, Saldenus realized. And he realized we would benefit by seeing it too.

> It is true that the joy of which we are speaking can be so abundant that it often stirs up the affections. However, this should not be viewed as normative. Much less should it be concluded that where this is lacking there would also be no spiritual joy in the heart. The seat of this joy is not in the affections, . . . but rather, in . . . the soul. . . . Such partakers will be filled with the greatest measure of joy even in the complete absence of all that is sensual. Peter speaks of this: "Though now you do not see him, yet believing, you rejoice with joy unspeakable and full of glory" (1 Pet. 1:8).[45]

What does he mean? When he says the stirring up of the affections shouldn't be viewed as normative, what he's saying is that the Bible doesn't tell us that it *has* to be what happens. We can't make a rule of something if the Bible doesn't. When he says the seat of this joy is the soul, not the affections, he's saying that this joy is much, much deeper than a feeling. We'll know it, and we may well feel it in our affections in some way, but what we feel is a reflection of something that goes far beyond our feelings.

Saldenus suggests three components of this joy that will help us to see that it's much deeper than a feeling. First, "it consists of a clearer and more distinct apprehension of the magnitude and preciousness of the suffering of Jesus Christ."[46] The supper proclaims the Lord's death, and we taste the truth of His body broken for us and His blood shed for the forgiveness of our sins. We grasp hold of the wonder of this Good News as we eat and drink at the Lord's table. The more we grasp hold of it, the more we rejoice in our Savior.

Second, "it consists in a greater and more certain peace of heart proceeding from and by way of an assured fellowship with the all-sufficient merits of Jesus Christ."[47] We hear those words "for you" in the supper, and feed upon Christ our sin offering. Our hearts are sprinkled with His blood as we drink of it in the cup. And in all this, we are assured that Christ's work is indeed for us.

Third, "it consists of a fuller peace and inner satisfaction and of a determination to obey in return."[48] We know more of the peace we have with God, and more of the satisfaction and delight in Jesus. And by this He changes us—this intimacy of communion is a transforming intimacy. And as we delight in Him more and more, we're more and more determined to be like Him. So our communion with Him causes us to desire more and more to obey Him. "Now he who keeps His commandments abides in Him, and He in him. And by this we know that He abides in us, by the Spirit whom He has given us." (1 John 3:24).

Joy in communion with Christ means seeing Jesus as ever more precious, knowing peace in Jesus and experiencing increasing delight in Jesus. Sometimes that joy will burst out in our affections. Other times that joy will remain a calm, deep peace and satisfaction, even in the midst of the storms of life.

So don't let these testimonies discourage you; let them whet your appetite. We can experience joy and bliss in communion with Christ in the supper. Draw near with expectation and faith. Remember, "we walk by faith, not by sight" (2 Corinthians 5:7). Jesus promises His presence at the supper. He promises communion with Him in His body and blood, and He invites us to come and eat and drink in faith. Sometimes our eyes will be opened and we'll see through the veil and be swept up in the experience of communion with Christ. Other times, we'll see only by faith. But it will be the same Jesus who meets us in the supper. And He'll be meeting us in the same glory, power and grace, whether we feel it or whether we merely grasp the hem of His garment in faith.

9

Every Spiritual Blessing

J ESUS IS OUR SALVATION. And Jesus is the source of every blessing included in our salvation. "The God and Father of our Lord Jesus Christ . . . has blessed us with every spiritual blessing in the heavenly places in Christ" (Ephesians 1:3). That's what it is to be "in Christ": United to Jesus, we share in everything that's His and everything that He's accomplished for us. And feeding upon Him in His body and blood in the supper, we feed upon the One in whom every spiritual blessing is found. There are blessings at the table of the Lord, because Jesus, the One in whom all blessing is found, is present in His supper.

So what are some of the blessings to be found in communion with Christ in His supper? We've already thought about some, like forgiveness of sins, being built up in unity with one another as Christ's Body, partaking in the divine nature, and the joy of communion, with Christ. But over the next two chapters, let's think about four more. In this chapter we're going to consider life and holiness, and in the next chapter, we'll think about healing and the outpouring of the Holy Spirit.

THE LIFE OF CHRIST
BY THE BREAD OF HEAVEN

Jesus promises life in eating His flesh and drinking His blood (John 6:53–58). Whoever "feeds on Me will live because of Me," says the Lord (verse 57). Life in Jesus isn't just life with Him in heaven after death and in the new heavens and new earth in the resurrection. No. Life in Jesus begins here and now. Eternal life is not just unending life; it's a type of life. A life in fellowship with the Triune God. A life indwelt by Jesus. A life of knowing the Father and the Son in the Spirit.

And so, as Jesus nourishes us now with His body and blood in His supper, He nourishes us with Himself as our life (see Colossians 3:4). All those who live in Him can say, "I have been crucified with Christ; it is no longer I who live, but Christ lives in me; and the life which I now live in the flesh I live by faith in the Son of God, who loved me and gave Himself for me" (Galatians 2:20).

As we feed on Christ in the supper, we are filled with Christ, who gives us life. Which is exactly why Jesus has come into the world: "I have come that they may have life, and that they may have it more abundantly" (John 10:10). The life Jesus offers to us is an abundant life, not a meager lack. When He declares His desire to give us such overflowing life, He then immediately tells us that He is the good Shepherd. And by that He tells us two things.

First, He tells us that "the good shepherd gives His life for the sheep" (John 10:11). So He tells us that by laying down His life in our place, He is giving us abundant life. Jesus, our good Shepherd, has died our death, and in return He fills us with His life. By His broken body and shed blood at the cross of Calvary, He has defeated death for us and won this new, abundant life for us. And now through His broken body and shed blood with which He feeds us at His table, He applies this victory to us and fills us more and more with His abundant life.

Second, in telling us He's the good Shepherd who gives us abundant life, He points us back to Psalm 23 and tells us that He is the Lord our Shepherd, and we shall not want (see Psalm 23:1). For my good Shepherd "makes me to lie down in green pastures; He leads me beside the still waters. He restores my soul" (Psalm 23:2–3). He provides an abundant life. When I'm weak with hunger and thirst, when I need to feed on rich pastures and drink of clear waters, I can draw near to my good Shepherd at the table He has prepared. When my soul needs to be refreshed and restored, I can run to Jesus and drink from His overflowing cup. When I walk through the valley of the shadow of death, I taste of His comfort in the supper, where He has promised He is with me.

As a pastor, I have seen that comfort of His presence at work in the supper so many times in so many people's lives. One Saturday night I received a phone call about a sudden and tragic death and went to see the family and pray with them. I didn't expect to see them first thing the next morning for the breaking of bread, but there they were. And as we gathered around the Lord's table, they lifted up their voices in faith-filled prayers of thanksgiving. They needed the Lord's comfort and strength in the wake of their tragedy, and they knew that the place to find it was where the Lord promised His presence—gathered in His house, with His people, eating and drinking at His table.

I can testify to that comfort in the supper too. A few years ago, I had a sudden period of severe depression that lasted for several months. I'd never experienced anything like that before, and I didn't understand at all what was happening. I couldn't concentrate on the sermons I heard in church or get much out of anything anyone said to me. I even found it incredibly difficult to focus my mind to pray or read the Bible. But even though I couldn't follow a sermon or derive any comfort from the well-meaning things friends said, I could come to the Lord's table each Lord's Day and cling to the presence of my Savior. I could hold on to the promise of those words, "This is My body, broken for you . . . this is My blood of the new covenant, shed for you for the forgiveness of sins." And I could find the truest comfort in the broken body and shed blood of the good Shepherd, who gave His life for me, one of His sheep, and rose again to carry me through the valley of the shadow of death. For a few months, from week to week, all I could do was cling to Jesus' Gospel words spoken over the bread and wine. Even though I couldn't concentrate, I could feel the broken bread and the chalice in my hands and taste them in my mouth, knowing the powerful promise that came with them. (And then, at a breaking of bread some months later, the Lord did something miraculous after the supper and healed me.)

Jesus, the good Shepherd, doesn't intend for us to limp along alone through the deathly valleys, the barren deserts and the dangerous, enemy-filled forests of life. He wants us to come to Him and find the abundance of His life. He is with us. He wants to meet us and feed us and fill us with more of Him and of His life at His table.

In John 15, Jesus tells us that He is the True Vine. "I am the vine, you are the branches. He who abides in Me, and I in him, bears much fruit; for without Me you can do nothing" (verse 5). We are to abide in the Vine and be filled with the life of the Vine. And it's only in abiding in the Vine, with the life of the Vine as our life, that we can be truly fruitful. So a fruitful life is an abiding life. And an abiding life is a life that drinks of the blood of Christ the Vine. For Jesus promised, whoever "eats My flesh and drinks My blood abides in Me, and I in him" (John 6:56).

This abiding, abundant, fruitful, eternal life is a life of knowing the Father and the Son (John 17:3). Not merely a life of knowing *about* the Father and the Son, but a life of intimate communion with the Trinity.

HOLY THINGS FOR HOLY PEOPLE

In the olden days (and in some parts of the world still) before Christ's people received Communion, the pastor would lift up the blessed bread and chalice and say, "Holy things for holy people." And then the whole church would respond and say, "There is One holy, even One Lord Jesus Christ, in whom are we to the glory of God the Father."[1] Jesus is the Holy One. He is our holiness, our sanctification (see 1 Corinthians 1:30). And so any holiness we have always comes from Him.

When I was growing up, the main thing at the front of the church when you walked in on a Sunday morning wasn't the pulpit, or a band warming up on the platform. It was the Communion table, carefully covered with a white cloth. As we waited for the service to begin, the deaconesses would place the chalice and paten (the plate used to carry the bread) on the table and cover them with a white veil. Both the veil and tablecloth had the same words embroidered on them, which were engraved on the chalice and paten too: *Holiness unto the Lord*. (This wasn't just a peculiarity of my local assembly; those words were found at Communion tables in Pentecostal churches all over the United Kingdom.) Going into church on the Lord's Day morning for the breaking-of-bread service, all eyes were drawn to the proclamation of the Lord's holiness at His table. And so, coming into church, we knew we had come to a holy meal where we would meet with a holy God.

But the Lord's holiness isn't just something to be displayed on white linens and a silver chalice. The Lord's holiness is to be displayed in His people who eat and drink of the Holy One in the supper. When we come to meet with our holy God at His table, it has a transformative effect on us. We can't encounter the Lord in His holiness and not be changed. Christ's people have always recognized that. An old chorus Pentecostals used to sing at the breaking of bread expresses this hunger for holiness that should draw us to the Lord's table:

> Taste the Bread of sweet Communion,
> Deeply drink the Covenant Wine.
> Bring our hearts in pure devotion
> To that Sacrifice of Thine.
> May the virtue in Thy body

Feed our souls with life divine,
And Thy blood with cleansing vigour
All our hearts and our lives refine.[2]

That's a prayer for holiness. A prayer for the Savior to sanctify through the supper. We come to the Lord's table longing for cleansing through the body and blood of Jesus and longing to be filled with His divine life and virtue. We don't want to leave here as we came, in Jesus' name!

But what is holiness? Well, think of those words that were on the cloth and the Communion cup: "Holiness to the Lord." Those words don't originate at the Communion table. They come from the Old Testament, from the plate of pure gold the high priest wore on his turban (see Exodus 28:36; 39:30). But what has the Israelite high priest got to do with us? Well, we have a High Priest too, and the Old Testament high priest points forward to our great High Priest, the Lord Jesus.

The high priest didn't say the words "Holiness to the Lord"; he wore them. They were placed on his person and connected to his work. So holiness isn't just connected to one thing that Jesus has done for us. Holiness comes from the Person of Jesus, the Holy One. And because it's Jesus the Holy One who has carried out the great high priestly work for us, everything He has done for us, and everything He does now in us, is holy. Holiness isn't one option among many for the Christian life. If we are united to Jesus and have Jesus living in us, then we're united to the Holy One, and His holiness dwells in us.

Now, this gold plate engraved with these holy words was the last thing made for the Tabernacle and its worship. When it was made, "All the work of the tabernacle of the tent of meeting was finished" (Exodus 39:32). So, once this inscription of "Holiness to the Lord" was ready, the Tabernacle was ready, and the first sacrifices could be offered on its altar. And when they were, "The cloud covered the tabernacle of meeting, and the glory of the LORD filled the tabernacle. And Moses was not able to enter the tabernacle of meeting, because the cloud rested above it, and the glory of the LORD filled the tabernacle" (Exodus 40:34–35). As soon as that proclamation of the Lord's holiness was ready, the time had come for God to flood the Tabernacle with His glorious presence. So, holiness shines out when God is present in His glory.

Now, in the New Testament, we're the Tabernacle—the Church is the new temple where God dwells. And so, as the Church is "filled with all the fullness of God" (Ephesians 3:19), it's filled with His holiness. When God's people encounter the presence of the Holy One, they encounter His holiness. True holiness is found only in the Lord alone. He calls us to be holy as He is holy (Leviticus 11:44; 1 Peter 1:15), but the only way we can truly be holy is with His holiness in us. So we need Christ as our holiness.

Holiness is found in the Lord Himself. So in the presence of the Holy One, we find His holiness. And that means "access to God's holiness depends on proximity to him."[3] It's the presence of the Lord that sanctifies His people. Although it might sound strange, the closer you get to God, the holier you are in His presence. We see that in Leviticus, where, as the theologian John Kleinig notes:

God did not keep his holiness to himself, nor did he use it to distance himself from his sinful people. Instead, he joined them on their earthly journey so that he could share his holiness with them. They did not sanctify themselves; he sanctified them. He made and kept them holy. They drew their holiness from him, and him only. . . . God communicated his holiness physically with his people through the holy things. By their access to the holy things the people shared in God's holiness.[4]

That might sound really strange, but it's not just in Leviticus. Remember when Isaiah saw the glory of the Lord filling the temple? When he came into the presence of the Lord, and heard the angels singing, "Holy, holy, holy," Isaiah was overwhelmed with the Lord's holiness. But how did the Lord purify Isaiah's unclean lips? He sent one of the seraphim "having in his hand a live coal which he had taken with the tongs from the altar" to touch Isaiah's lips (Isaiah 6:5–7). A coal that had touched the sacrifice on the altar now touched Isaiah's lips. It was through a physical touch that the Lord communicated His holiness to the prophet. And not just any physical touch. A touch from the altar where atonement was made.

And we, too, have our lips touched by holiness from the altar where atonement was made. Only, our lips aren't touched by an angel carrying coal. Our lips are touched by the holy body and blood of our holy Savior, who was lifted up on the cross in our place as the once-and-for-all sacrifice for sin. Isaiah's lips were touched by a coal from the altar of the temple that pointed forward to the altar of the cross. But our lips are touched by the Lord Himself from the true altar of the once-for-all, perfect sacrifice of the Lamb of God who takes away the sins of the world. And not only are our lips touched by holiness from the true altar, but we eat and drink and are fed with the holiness of the Holy One. As we are fed with the body and blood of Christ, we partake in Him of "saving sanctification."[5]

Now, notice this. Our true holiness is found in Jesus, the One whom we eat. We keep coming back to His table, day after day and week after week, to feed on Him again and again. We often wish we could just be zapped with holiness—that God would just snap His fingers and *voilà!* But that's not how it works. We don't suddenly get sanctification. No! We get Jesus, and *He* is our sanctification. And although we're united to Jesus when we turn from our sin and put our trust in Him, He continues to build us up in Him and strengthen that union throughout our lives, so that we are conformed more and more to His likeness and more and more of His holiness is seen in us. As we meet with Jesus in His Word (John 17:17), by His Spirit (2 Thessalonians 2:13) and at His table (1 Corinthians 10:16), He sanctifies us as He molds us more and more into His image.

So sanctification isn't a onetime thing; it's ongoing. And it *will* be until we see Him face-to-face, and then we shall be like Him (1 John 3:2). But in the meantime, as we await that day when we'll be raised with Him in glory, the process of sanctification continues in our lives in two major ways: in dying to sin (*mortification*), and in living to righteousness (*vivification*). In the supper, Jesus is at work in both these ways: putting sin to death and strengthening His new, resurrection life in us.

THE POWER OF THE CROSS

When we eat Christ's flesh and drink His blood, we meet with Him in the power of His atoning death on the cross.

But Jesus didn't just die in our place on the cross. We also died in Him. "We have been united together in the likeness of His death . . . our old man was crucified with Him, that the body of sin might be done away with, that we should no longer be slaves of sin" (Romans 6:5–6). Therefore, we are not to "let sin reign" in our mortal bodies that we "should obey it in its lusts" (Romans 6:12). United to Jesus, we have died and our "life is hidden with Christ in God" (Colossians 3:3). "Therefore," we must "put to death [our] members which are on the earth: fornication, uncleanness, passion, evil desire, and covetousness, which is idolatry" (Colossians 3:5). We have been united to Christ in His death, and now the power of that death needs to be killing sin in us. That's the mortification side of sanctification: putting sin to death.

Paul wrote to the Romans about the vital need for this outworking of the power of the cross in our lives: "If you live according to the flesh you will die; but if by the Spirit you put to death the deeds of the body, you will live" (Romans 8:13). Mortification isn't something that happens invisibly— we're called to live in this power of our union with Christ in His death and be active in putting our sinful deeds to death. Paul is writing to Christians who have been freed from sin's condemnation. He's writing to those who have had their sins forgiven and have been clothed with Christ for righteousness. Yet he makes it very clear that we need to give attention to putting sin to death in our lives now, by the power of the Holy Spirit, and in light of the cross and our union with Jesus. John Owen famously summarized what Paul has to say: "Always be killing sin, or it will be killing you!"[6]

So how does the supper help us put sin to death in our lives? Well, notice something about each of the Scriptures above that tell us about the need for killing sin: *In none of them are we left to do it alone.* It's because we've been united to Jesus in His death and our old man has been crucified with Him that we're no longer under sin's slavery, and are free not to let it reign in our lives (see Romans 6:5–6, 12). It's because we've died with Jesus and our life is now hidden in Him that we can put sinful deeds to death in our lives here on earth (see Colossians 3:3–5). It's because we have the Holy Spirit living in us that we can, through Him, put the sinful deeds of the body to death (see Romans 8:13). It's only by being united to Jesus and filled with His Spirit that we can do this. It's only through the power of Christ's cross and the power of the Holy Spirit that we can be killing sin day by day.

That's exactly what we encounter in the supper. We eat His body and drink His blood—which are filled with the Spirit through whom Jesus offered Himself up on the cross for us (see Hebrews 9:14). And so, as we receive Jesus' Spirit-filled, sin-defeating body and blood in faith, they weaken sin in us. As Stephen Charnock put it, "As Christ upon the cross expiated sin, so Christ in the supper mortifies sin by His Spirit, and purges those iniquities which are as a veil between the face of God and the joy of our souls."[7]

Jesus died for sin to die in us. He died so that we'd no longer live for sin, but for Him. And so as we proclaim the Lord's death in the supper and feed upon His once-for-all sacrifice for sin, we become enemies of sin. We eat and drink of the sin-killing power of the cross, and we go from the table in that sin-killing power. Now, this isn't magic. The Bible calls upon us to kill sin in our lives (through Jesus and by the Spirit). Fighting and killing sin in our lives can be painful and the battle can be hard. But by His cross and resurrection, Jesus has already won the victory. And so, as we eat His body and drink His blood in faith, we are partaking of His triumph. And going out from the table, filled more and more with the sin-vanquishing Savior in the mighty power of His cross of victory, we're enabled more and more to rely on the mighty power of His blood and see His blood-bought victory out-worked in our lives.

The Holy Spirit mortifies sin in us when He brings Christ's cross into our hearts "by faith, and gives communion with Christ in His death, and fellowship in His sufferings."[8] And that's exactly what's going on in the Lord's Supper. So this table of Communion is also a table where sin is being put to death, Sunday after Sunday, as we eat and drink in humble, repentant faith. But we must always keep our eyes on the true Sin-Killer. It's not the supper that saves; it's the Savior whom we meet in the supper. It's not the supper that triumphs over sin; it's the crucified and risen Jesus who gives us His body and blood to eat there at the table. So we need to keep our eyes fixed on Christ in faith as we eat and drink in the sacrament. Keep your eyes on Jesus as your victory and His broken body and shed blood as your sin-killing power. "Let faith gaze upon Christ as He is set forth crucified and dying for us. Look upon Him under the weight of our sins, pray-ing, bleeding, and dying. . . . Bring Him in that condition into your heart by faith. Apply His blood so shed to your corruptions."[9]

As you come to Him in faith at the table, look on Him in His sin-defeating power. And as you go from the table, re-member that He dwells in those who eat His flesh and drink His blood in faith, so you go with your Sin-Killer still abiding in you. Both at the table as you eat, and then throughout the week, trusting in the One whose body and blood you have eaten, "set your faith upon Christ for the killing of your sin. His blood is the great sovereign remedy for sin-sick souls. Live in the light of Christ's great work, and you will die a conqueror."[10]

The Bible says, "Those who are Christ's have crucified the flesh with its passions and desires. If we live in the Spirit, let us also walk in the Spirit" (Galatians 5:24–25). In the supper, we taste of the cross. And through the power of Christ's cross, joined to Him our sinful flesh is crucified and our sins are mortified.

Bring the sins you're battling with to Jesus' powerful blood as you drink of it in the supper. I've seen again and again, and heard testimony after testimony, of those who found the power they needed in their fight against sin in the supper. They've found it in the supper, because they've found the sin-defeating body and blood of the Savior there. And His promise is for you too.

You can't kill sin by yourself. Only through Jesus' death for you and His Spirit living in you can you be killing sin. So come, bring your struggle to the supper, and you'll find there the victory of the Savior. Come to the cup in faith, saying:

Lord, I am an unrighteous creature, but here is justifying blood; my heart is unholy, but here sanctifying blood; my soul is wounded, but here healing blood; my lusts are strong, but here mortifying blood; my heart is hard, but here softening blood; my affections are dead, but here quickening blood; my love is cold, but here heart-warming blood. O my glorious bleeding Lamb, if You are willing, You can make me clean. O say to me, as You did to the leper, "I am willing, be clean." Surely Your blood is more able to save me, than my sins are to destroy me.[11]

He is willing. His death on the cross for you proves it. So come and drink His blood and be clean. And by His blood be killing sin so it won't be killing you.

THE POWER OF THE RESURRECTION

But sanctification doesn't stop with putting sin to death. Jesus didn't just come to defeat sin. He came to give us new life. When we meet with Jesus in the supper, it's the risen, glorified Savior with whom we meet. He is the Lamb who was slain, but who is now alive! And as He feeds us with His risen, glorified and ascended body and blood, He fills us with more and more of the power of His resurrection life. The risen Lamb dwells in us and we dwell in Him.

Now each of us can say with Paul, "I have been crucified with Christ; it is no longer I who live, but Christ lives in me; and the life which I now live in the flesh I live by faith in the Son of God, who loved me and gave Himself for me" (Galatians 2:20). Christ lives in us, and we live now by faith in Him. This is the new life to which we have been raised by the Holy Spirit through faith in Jesus. This is the abundant life Jesus has promised us (see John 10:10)—His resurrection life in us.

So as we feed on our crucified and risen Savior in the supper, in faith we look to Him as our Source of abundant life, resurrection power and joy-filled holiness. Jesus is full of all this for us, "for it pleased the Father that in [Jesus] all the fullness should dwell" (Colossians 1:19). And this isn't a fullness that will get any less full. If I have a full glass of water on a hot summer's day, the moment I take a sip, it isn't full anymore. So I have to think about how to make it last as long as I need it to. I need to ration out my sips so it won't run out. But Jesus isn't like that. Not at all. His fullness is a perfect fullness that can never be diminished.

The Puritan Isaac Ambrose got very excited about this. "Christ is full," he exclaimed, "and ever shall be full to the brim! . . . He overflows and fills all his saints: He is the well-head or fountain, which is not only full itself, but springs and flows over to the filling of the streams below it."[12] He does that so often through His holy Supper. We behold Jesus in His wondrous fullness of life and holiness for us, and we go to Him at the table where we eat and drink, filled with faith, "and so draw forth the efficacy of Christ in the sacrament."[13] (It might help you to meditate on Colossians 1:19–20 as you wait to receive the elements at the Lord's Supper, and pray those verses back to the Father as you eat and drink, saying: "Thank You that it pleased You, Father, that in Jesus all the fullness should dwell, and that by Him You reconcile all things to Yourself, through the blood of His cross.") When that's how we come to the table, we go home from feeding on Jesus in His fullness in the supper with our faith strengthened, our hearts warmed, our graces nourished, our corruptions weakened and our assurance heightened.[14] We go home from the supper living more and more in the power of Christ's resurrection life in us.

Therefore, not only does the Savior who died for us put sin to death in us as we partake of Him in the supper with faith, but the Savior who rose for us is at work to empower us to walk in His ways and obey His commands. Sanctification isn't just about sinning less or overcoming temptation more. As we feed upon our risen Savior—both in the supper and as we spend time with Him in His Word—He is at work in us to conform us more and more to His image.

YOU ARE WHAT YOU EAT

When we feed on Jesus, we become more and more like Jesus. As Leo the Great put it, all the way back in the fifth century: "Our partaking of the Body and Blood of Christ tends only to make us become what we eat."[15] As we eat His flesh and drink His blood, we abide in Jesus and He abides in us (see John 6:56). And abiding in us, He transforms us into His likeness from the inside out.

According to Jesus, it's what comes from the inside that defiles. "What comes out of a man, that defiles a man. For from within, out of the heart of men, proceed evil thoughts, adulteries, fornications, murders, thefts, covetousness, wickedness, deceit, lewdness, an evil eye, blasphemy, pride, foolishness. All these evil things come from within and defile a man" (Mark 7:20–23). It's not sinful actions that make a sinner; it's sinners who sin. And the same goes for holiness. "A good man out of the good treasure of his heart brings forth good; and an evil man out of the evil treasure of his heart brings forth evil. For out of the abundance of the heart his mouth speaks" (Luke 6:45). Just as evil comes from within, so does good. But "no one is good but One, that is, God" (Matthew 19:17; Mark 10:18; Luke 18:19). So true goodness—true holiness—isn't something we can produce by ourselves. Yes, it comes from within. But only as Jesus abides within. "Abide in Me," says Jesus, "and I in you. As the branch cannot bear fruit of itself, unless it abides in the vine, neither can you, unless you abide in Me" (John 15:4).

As we feed upon Him in faith in the supper, Jesus abides in us. Our Bread of Heaven isn't broken down and conformed to our way of life. No. As we eat Him, He builds us up into His life.

> Nothing is more intimately related to the Lord Christ than His assumed human nature, His flesh and His blood, with which He has personally united Himself; however, nothing comes closer to us humans than what we eat and drink, since it permeates our innermost being. Accordingly, since the Lord Christ wanted to unite us and Himself to the deepest and most precise degree, to that end it pleased Him that we receive His true body and blood by means of the consecrated bread and wine.[16]

He feeds us with Himself and in that way unites us to Himself in the deepest, most intimate way. And so through His body and blood:

> We are most intimately joined together with Christ Himself through the nature which He has inseparably . . . united to Himself, and through Christ we are united with the Father. For through the bread we are united with the body of Christ, and through the body with Christ Himself, and through Christ with the Father. Thus we are made partakers with the Father, the Son, and the Holy Spirit.[17]

That is God's great plan for us in Jesus: to bring us into this communion with the Trinity so that we are partakers of the divine nature (see 2 Peter 1:4). In this eternal communion we are being conformed to His image and built up in His likeness. With faith and a humble heart, we eat of the Holy One in the supper, and He transforms us from within to be holy like Him. As we behold the glory of the Lord God in the face of Jesus Christ when we eat and drink of His body and blood, we are "transformed into the same image from glory to glory" (2 Corinthians 3:18).

10

The Power of
His Presence

A S WE SAW AT THE BEGINNING of the last
chapter, when we encounter Jesus in His supper, we
feed upon the One in whom every spiritual blessing is found.
When we come to the Lord's table we are blessed, because
Jesus is there. We've already thought about the blessings of
forgiveness, new life and holiness, which we find only in Jesus.
But there are other blessings found in Him too. Blessings far
beyond what we could ask or imagine. Sometimes in the supper we encounter His blessing in incredibly powerful ways
we might not have been expecting. Sometimes at His table,
He heals. And sometimes at the supper, He powerfully pours
out His Spirit.

THE MEDICINE OF IMMORTALITY

The first time I read an old Pentecostal book that mentioned "healing in the Cup," I was a bit confused. Growing up, I knew from the way we celebrated the breaking of bread that something very important was going on. But then I'd gone to university, and read a lot of books telling me what (the authors thought) Evangelicals and Pentecostals really believed about the supper. Apparently, it wasn't really all that significant, just a reminder of what Jesus had done two thousand years ago, the same way many other things could remind us of that glorious truth. But then I started reading old Pentecostal books and discovered a very different story. The centrality of the breaking of bread in Pentecostal worship when I was growing up made a lot more sense in light of what the Pentecostal writers actually wrote.

After discovering healing in the cup in an old book, I mentioned it to a very elderly lady in church while we were chatting after the service one Sunday morning. "Oh yes!" she said. "We never used to pray for people to be healed on a Sunday morning, because they would just get healed as they ate and drank at the breaking of bread." Then she started to tell me the testimonies of how she and her family and friends had been healed of all sorts of sicknesses and injuries at the very moment of eating the blessed bread or drinking from the cup. "Then we started calling people up specifically for prayer for healing on Sunday mornings and people seemed to forget that Jesus could heal us in the supper," she said.

More recently, there has been a renewed interest in healing in the Lord's Supper, but unfortunately, some of the things that have been written about it are a bit confusing. So let's straighten things out and make sure we understand what healing at the table really does mean.

First, there is healing in the supper, because Jesus the Healer is present in the supper. It's not eating bread and drinking wine while thinking about Jesus that heals. It's Jesus Himself who heals. The healing power of the supper isn't in anything we do when we take Communion; the healing power of the supper is in Jesus, who meets us in all His grace there.

When we meet with Jesus, there isn't something special that we need to do to unleash His healing power. Jesus isn't a healing mechanism; He's the Healer. And He is full of compassion, love and mercy to those who bring their needs to Him. When Jesus was on His way to raise Jairus's daughter from the dead, a woman came to Him for healing. She knew that He was the Healer. And she knew that she didn't need to get a half-hour appointment or go through an elaborate ritual. She knew that all she needed to do to receive a full healing from Jesus was touch the edge of His clothing, "for she said to herself, 'If only I may touch His garment, I shall be made well'" (Matthew 9:21). And she was. She laid hold of the hem of Christ's garment, and the Lord turned to her and said, "Be of good cheer, daughter; your faith has made you well" (Matthew 9:22). A mere touch of the hem of Christ's coat, together with her faith in Him, healed a sickness that had lasted for twelve years! Not because there was any power in the coat, but because Christ the Healer was wearing the coat. To touch the hem of His garment was to touch the Healer Himself.

She wasn't the only one. Again and again, sick people were brought to Jesus "and begged Him that they might only touch the hem of His garment. And as many as touched it were made perfectly well" (Matthew 14:36). And "wherever He entered, into villages, cities, or the country, they laid the sick in the marketplaces, and begged Him that they might just touch the hem of His garment. And as many as touched Him were made well" (Mark 6:56). Jesus could heal through the mere touch of the hem of His garment.

In the Lord's Supper, He draws even closer to us than that. At the table, we don't just get a fleeting touch of the hem of His garment. He gives us something much more wonderful and much more powerful. He feeds us with His body and blood. We get ahold of His very body given for us, and we don't just touch it. We eat it. In the supper, the Healer gets as close to us as it is possible to get.

So if the merest touch of the hem of His garment could heal an illness that had baffled the doctors for over a decade, how much more can He do for us when we eat and drink of the Healer Himself? When we gather at the Lord's table, we're not gathering to remember an absent Savior. Not at all! We're gathering to meet with the living, risen, glorified Savior who has triumphed over death through His death and resurrection in our place. We're gathering to meet with the ascended Savior who ever lives to intercede for us before the Father—the great High Priest who pleads His blood for us in all our needs, including our weaknesses and sicknesses. We're gathering to meet with the exalted Lord, who pours out the Spirit from the Father, filling us with His comfort, His peace and His love, and distributing His gifts of healings. We're not just meeting with someone who happens to be able to heal. We're meeting with the God who took on our flesh to live for us, fulfill all righteousness for us, die in our place, rise victorious from the grave having triumphed over all His and our enemies and who continually applies His great and full salvation to us through His intercession and by His Spirit. Jesus is *for us*. And He gives Himself *to us* in the supper. That's coming far closer than the mere touch of a hem of a garment. If you could physically hold the hem of Christ's garment in your hands, how strongly you'd believe. If you could hear Him standing beside you praying for you, how much assurance you'd have of the answer to that prayer. In the supper, Jesus doesn't merely draw alongside us so we can grasp hold of the hem of His garment or hear His intercession for us. As you feel the bread on your tongue and the wine on your lips, know that Jesus is drawing as near as can be. Know that Jesus is coming to dwell in you. He's coming to strengthen your union with Him and fill you even more with Himself. As you taste this bread and this wine, you are tasting the Medicine of Immortality, because you are tasting Jesus.

Second, to understand the place of healing at the Lord's Supper, we have to realize that receiving the supper does not *guarantee* healing. The supper isn't a mechanical thing. It's not like taking your vitamins every day to stay healthy. We can take vitamins automatically; it's part of the habits of a daily routine. But we should not treat the body and blood of Christ like that. We shouldn't take the Lord's Supper on autopilot, thinking it will guarantee health and healing.

We've already seen how we need to prepare ourselves before we come to the Lord's table. We need to acknowledge and confess our sins and run to Jesus for His forgiveness. We need to discern the Lord's body, and none of that can be done on autopilot.

Discerning the Lord's body is how we know there is healing at the table. Unless we see it is Jesus who is there, we won't see the true source of healing in the supper. Healing isn't found by simply receiving Communion without recognizing and revering the presence of Jesus.

This recognition that it's the blood of Jesus Himself in the supper should fill us with confidence as we drink from the cup. Early Pentecostals were disturbed as they saw other Christians start to abandon the common cup out of fear of sickness, instead of trusting in what Christ had instituted in His Word. "We cannot understand," they said, "how any true Christian can see danger in the members using the same cup at the Lord's table. We are partaking of and communing with Christ, who is Life and Health. How can we partake of Life and Health and death and sickness at the same time, from the same source? . . . To say that there is danger is nothing but to belittle the value of Christ's atonement."[1]

Yet, even when we recognize the closeness of the presence of Christ the Healer in the supper, that still doesn't guarantee healing. We are to come to Him in faith, trusting fully in Him and His grace for us. But we don't come presuming.

Jesus hasn't invited us to the table to be healed, though He does heal there. He has invited us to the table to eat His flesh and drink His blood, proclaiming His death until He comes. He has invited us to the table to meet with Him. And when He meets with us there, He may well choose to heal. But if you come to the table looking for healing instead of looking for Jesus, you've come looking for the wrong thing. Seek the Giver, not the gifts. Seek the Healer, not the healing. And seeking Jesus, we find every spiritual blessing in Him.

TESTIMONIES OF HEALING
AT THE SUPPER

In the village of Machen in Monmouthshire (in south Wales), there lived a man called Mr. W. J. Jones, who had been in terrible agony from tuberculosis for three years. In 1915, some friends invited him to their Pentecostal church in a nearby village. So on the Lord's Day morning, Mr. Jones went to the breaking of bread in Cross Keys. Mr. Jones tells us that the pastor of the assembly, Tom Mercy, went to the Communion table and said, "If we would eat in faith, Christ in us would be life and health to our bodies." Mr. Jones thought to himself, *That is just what I need, a healthy body.* He would later testify, "When the bread was offered to me, I ate in faith, and Glory to God, the Lord just touched me! I felt His touch, and Glory to His Name, I was made perfectly whole! Today there is not a healthier or stronger man in Machen." Mr. Jones said that he would never forget the presence and the glory of the Lord that he encountered as he ate and drank at the Lord's table that Sunday in Cross Keys. "Jesus is the . . . mighty deliverer and He made me whole." [2]

Miss N. Kennedy moved from Britain to Canada, where she met some Pentecostals and was baptized in the Spirit. She started attending church with these Pentecostal friends, and joined the Calvary Temple in Winnipeg. And there, one Sunday morning at the breaking of bread, she encountered Christ in His healing power. The Lord healed her of anemia as she ate and drank at His table. [3]

In Oklahoma, a woman lay dying of tuberculosis. Wanting to receive the Lord's Supper one last time, she called for the local Pentecostal pastor, Brother Beall, who brought a few other saints from the church so they could celebrate the sacrament together. Gathering in the little house where the sick woman lay, they held a simple breaking of bread. But when the woman received Communion, she was no longer on her deathbed, for the Lord healed her when He met with her in the supper.[4]

Notice this in each of these testimonies: Mr. Jones, Miss Kennedy, and the woman on her deathbed in Oklahoma had simply gone to the breaking of bread to meet with Jesus in His supper. They went seeking the Giver, and when they met Him, He bestowed His gift of healing as well.

WHEN HEALING DOESN'T COME

We might not be healed at the table. And that's okay. Because the Lord has not said in His Word, "Is anyone among you sick? Let him take Communion for healing." No! What the Lord tells the sick to do in His Word is something else:

> Is anyone among you sick? Let him call for the elders of the church, and let them pray over him, anointing him with oil in the name of the Lord. And the prayer of faith will save the sick, and the Lord will raise him up.
>
> James 5:14–15

For every testimony of healing at the Lord's Supper, there are dozens more of healing through the elders of the church anointing with oil. In His grace, as Christ meets us at His table, many times He heals. Often when we aren't expecting it. Healing at the table is, in many ways, a side effect of the presence of Jesus.

In my years as a pastor, I've seen people healed at the table, and I've seen people who've come faithfully to the table every Sunday, with faith in the presence of Jesus, who haven't been healed. But they haven't been disappointed in the supper. Because the reason they came was to meet with Jesus.

Jesus heals. He is the same yesterday, today and forever. And just as He showed His compassion and mercy on sick people who came to Him during His earthly ministry, He shows His compassion and mercy on sick people who come to Him today. But Jesus is never constrained to heal. He does heal, but not always. Sometimes He has another plan. Yet we know that we can trust Him and find strength and nourishment in Him, no matter what our circumstances.

Some believers will find healing at the Lord's table; others will meet Him there in His gracious and compassionate, sustaining power to carry them through days of sickness and suffering. They will find Him there as the One who shelters and sustains them in the valley of the shadow of death. Both those who are healed and those who are sustained meet the same Jesus in the supper. And His presence is just as powerful for both.

Eventually, for all of us, the day will come when we will not be healed in this life, because it is time for the Lord to take us home. We shouldn't think that Communion "isn't working" if there is death instead of healing. For the "job" of the supper isn't to heal, but to convey Christ to us. And while Christ is indeed the mighty and gracious Healer, He also uses death to call His people home to His presence.

The woman on her deathbed in Oklahoma sent for the pastor so she could taste of the Lord's goodness in the supper one more time before He took her home. (It just turned out that the Lord had other plans.) Christians down through the centuries have done the same.

Back in the seventeenth century, Jeremy Taylor, the Protestant Bishop of Down, Connor and Dromore (in what is now Northern Ireland), wrote that it is the pastor's duty "to invite sick and dying persons to the holy sacrament" in order that they may receive "into their souls the pledges of immortality, and may appear before God their Father in the union and with the impresses and likeness of their Elder Brother [the Lord Jesus]."[5] Jesus meets us in the supper as a way of preparing us for dying (not only at the moment we die, but all through our lives). He grants us His presence in the sacrament to get us ready to depart this world to be forever in His presence. And so, taking Communion to the sick and dying is part of the Church's care of the sick and dying. Those who are too sick to come to church are still part of the Church, and they still need the Church to bring the supper to them, to meet with Jesus there. For "in this sacrament," as Matthew Henry put it, we receive from the death of Christ "grace to prepare us for death, and to carry us safely and comfortably through the dark and dismal valley."[6] (Of course, Jesus will be faithful to us at the moment of death, whether we've just received the sacrament or not.)

But even the dying must eat of the supper in faith. While encouraging them in their duty of love to take the supper to the sick, Jeremy Taylor also reminded pastors that "to infuse the chalice into the cold lips [of the unconscious] cannot relieve the soul."[7] The sacrament isn't magic.

It's not bread and wine that brings us comfort in the hour of death. It's Jesus, who meets us in bread and wine. "What is your only comfort in life and death?" asks the *Heidelberg Catechism*. And its answer is:

That I am not my own, but belong with body and soul, both in life and in death, to my faithful Saviour Jesus Christ. He has fully paid for all my sins with His precious blood, and has set me free from all the power of the devil. He also preserves me in such a way that without the will of my heavenly Father not a hair can fall from my head; indeed, all things must work together for my salvation. Therefore, by His Holy Spirit He also assures me of eternal life and makes me heartily willing and ready from now on to live for Him.[8]

This comfort of belonging to Jesus, with all the glorious reality of what Jesus has done for us, is the very comfort we receive when He comes to us in the supper. Jesus Himself is our only comfort in life and death. And to taste again of that comfort on our way to death is a very good thing.

Of course, it's not just as we draw our final breath that we need that great comfort in Christ. Throughout this life, we will know times of suffering and hardship. And in those times, Christ will comfort, strengthen and sustain us through His presence in the supper.

Ultimately, the Lord will not merely prepare us through His presence in the supper for death, but for the resurrection. The Bread of Heaven is not just Medicine for the sick. He is the Medicine of Immortality.[9] And He has promised, "Whoever eats My flesh and drinks My blood has eternal life, and I will raise him up at the last day" (John 6:54). Eating Christ's flesh and drinking His blood—partaking of our Savior in His Supper—prepares our bodies for that last day, when Jesus will raise us from the dead and transform our weak and decaying bodies to be glorious and incorruptible. As Johann Gerhard wrote, "It is impossible that the same ones who have been nourished with the body and blood of our Lord—with the greatest of meals—would remain in the grave!"[10]

DRINKING OF THE SPIRIT

Jesus is the Christ—the Anointed One. *Christ* is simply our English version of the Greek word for "Anointed One."

Have you ever been anointed with oil? You couldn't just sit there by yourself in an empty room and suddenly become anointed. No. To be anointed always requires two other things: someone to do the anointing, and something to be anointed with. That's what the title *Christ* is telling us. Every time we use the title Christ, we're being reminded that Jesus is the Anointed One. God the Father has anointed His incarnate Son with the Holy Spirit. So, every time we use the title Christ, it's pointing us to the Triune God: The Anointer has anointed His Son with the Anointing (the Holy Spirit). The Father has poured out the perfect full anointing of the Holy Spirit on Jesus. Jesus is perfectly full of the Spirit.

We see this dramatically displayed in the waters of the Jordan when Jesus is baptized (see Matthew 3:16–17). But He isn't only the Anointed One in that moment. No. Jesus is always full of the Holy Spirit (see Luke 4:1). He was conceived by the power of the Holy Spirit in the womb of the virgin Mary (see Luke 1:35), and He offered Himself up without spot to God on the cross through the eternal Spirit (see Hebrews 9:14). The Spirit unites us to Christ so that we are one spirit with Him (see 1 Corinthians 6:17), and Christ has received the promise of the Holy Spirit from the Father to pour out on His people (see Acts 2:33). Jesus is the Spirit-Anointed Spirit-Baptizer.

Now, we need to understand this: Jesus is not just the perfect example of the Spirit-filled human being. It's true, He is filled with the Spirit in His human nature, but there's a big difference between Jesus and us. We are filled with the Spirit, whom Jesus pours out, but Jesus isn't filled with the Spirit poured out by someone else. He's filled with the Spirit with whom He and His Father are one. Jesus is God the Son, and the Holy Spirit proceeds from the Father through Him eternally. That's a very big difference between how Jesus relates to the Holy Spirit and how we do. This has always been an important truth for Christians to understand. Cyril of Alexandria explained it this way:

> When the Only Begotten Word of God became man, he remained, even so, God, having absolutely all that the Father has with the sole exception of being the Father. He had as his very own the Holy Spirit which is from him and within him essentially and so he brought about divine signs, and even when he became man he remained God and accomplished miracles in his very own power through the Spirit.[11]

Jesus didn't just do wondrous works by the Spirit in the same way a human being like us could through the Spirit's gift of the working of miracles. No. Jesus has the Spirit within Him in a way far beyond any of us. And that means that not only is the body of Jesus filled with His divine life because He is God the Son, but His body is also perfectly full of the Spirit of the God who "does not give the Spirit by measure" (see John 3:34).

That glorious truth doesn't put the fullness of the Spirit beyond your reach. By faith, we are united to Jesus by the

Holy Spirit. We are one with Jesus and share in all that is His. The Bible describes our union with Christ as a marriage. And when you get married, one of the promises you make is "all that I am I give to you, and all that I have I share with you." That's the sort of union we have with the Lord Jesus. He gives us all that He is and shares with us all that He has. He is the well-beloved Son of the Father, and He brings us into that relationship, to share in His love for the Father and the Father's love for Him, as well-beloved sons in the well-beloved Son. He takes our unrighteousness and clothes us in His perfect righteousness. He is the Anointed One, and in Him we share in His anointing. He has the fullness of the Spirit without measure, and He pours out the fullness of His Spirit upon us. It is because Jesus has the Spirit in a way beyond what's possible for a mere human being that we can be united to Him by the Spirit and filled with His Spirit.

Not only are His flesh and blood perfectly Spirit-filled flesh and blood, but by feeding us with His perfectly Spirit-filled flesh and blood, He can fill us with the Spirit, pour out the gifts of the Spirit and produce in us more of the fruit of the Spirit, as He meets with us in the supper. As the Church sang in praise to Jesus back in the fourth century:

> In your bread is hidden the Spirit which cannot be eaten.
> In your wine dwells the fire that cannot be drunk.
> Spirit in your bread, fire in your wine:
> It is a distinct wonder that our lips have received!
>
> Behold the fire and the Spirit in the womb which bore
>   you.
> Behold the fire and the Spirit in the river in which you
>   were baptized.

Fire and Spirit are in our baptism.
Fire and the Holy Spirit are in the bread and the cup.[12]

Sometimes people get the funny idea that the gifts of the Spirit and the table of the Lord are opposites. Maybe they've encountered a seriousness about the supper in more formal church services and spiritual gifts in places that don't seem to come to the table as often. Unfortunately, we can end up creating divisions between things the Lord has put together. After all, it's in the same few chapters near the end of 1 Corinthians where we get the biggest bit of teaching about both celebrating the supper *and* moving in the gifts.

Not only do the gifts of the Spirit and the table of the Lord belong together, in the same Church, at the same service, but Jesus offers His gift-giving Spirit in His Spirit-filled body and blood *at* the table. Now, that's not the only way Jesus pours out the Spirit. We have plenty of examples in the Bible of people receiving the Spirit while praying (see Acts 2:4; 4:31), as the Word is being proclaimed (see Acts 10:44; 11:15), at a baptism (see Acts 9:17–18; 19:5–6), while being prayed for (see Acts 8:15; 9:17), or by the laying on of hands (see Acts 8:17; Acts 19:6). So the pouring out of the Spirit and the Spirit's giving of His gifts isn't something that only happens at Communion. But it does happen at Communion. And that might be a place where we're not expecting it quite so much. We need to know about it, so we can pray for it, long for it and be ready when it happens.

When we come to Christ at His table, and drink the cup, we are "all given the one Spirit to drink" (1 Corinthians 12:13 NIV). How? Because Jesus' blood is Spirit-filled blood. It is "light, life, fire, and living water."[13] And so, drinking of the

Spirit as we drink of Christ's blood, we can know the effective working of the Spirit in us. For we drink His Spirit-filled blood "as water which wells up and speaks within [us]."[14]

THE BAPTISM AND GIFTS OF THE SPIRIT

When the Pentecostal revival broke out in the Netherlands at the beginning of the twentieth century, many people in Amsterdam were baptized in the Spirit while they were partaking of the Lord's Supper.[15] The same thing happened in the UK. One Sunday evening at a breaking of bread in Coventry, "as the brethren were serving the wine, the power descended and one of the brethren, as he stood by the Communion Table, was baptized with the Holy Spirit." Three women in the assembly were also baptized in the Spirit as they drank from the cup.[16] At a Sunday morning breaking of bread in Enfield, although there was "little fervency and no unusual stirring of the emotions" during the praise and worship, suddenly, as people began to eat and drink of the Lord's Supper:

> God interrupted the meeting by opening the windows of heaven and pouring us out such a blessing! The place was simply deluged with the mighty power of God, with nearly everyone under the power of the Spirit. One brother received an extraordinary baptism, and several were prostrated beneath the power.[17]

The testimony of a breaking of bread in Selly Oak, Birmingham, was that "the presence of the Lord fills the place" for "truly the Cup of the Lord's people is full and running over. He gives without measure to those who love Him,"[18] as one woman discovered when she drank from the chalice and was baptized in the Spirit.

At the Cardiff Temple, "it was obvious that the power of the Lord was present" at the breaking of bread, as a fifteen-year-old girl received the baptism of the Spirit while partaking of the sacrament.[19] In London, those who were present at a memorable breaking of bread in East Ham (where fifteen hundred people sat around the Lord's table), said they "will never forget it," for "many received the Baptism of the Holy Ghost" as they ate and drank of the supper. And many "bodies were healed" too.[20]

In America, Aimee Semple McPherson received a fresh outpouring of the Spirit at the Lord's table the day after she was baptized in the Spirit. Here's how she described what happened to her:

> I was taking the Lord's Supper for the first time when I went down . . . under the power. [She experienced] an exceeding weight of glory. . . . I was lost again with Jesus whom my soul loved, and speaking in tongues, and shaking under the power.[21]

Aimee said that, as she was eating and drinking at the Lord's table, the Comforter filled her with joy and with love for Jesus. We can be filled with the Spirit at the table, too, and know His joy and peace and love poured out in our hearts. It's no wonder that the Singaporean Pentecostal theologian Simon Chan encourages people to realize that "Holy Communion is the most appropriate occasion for a fresh in-filling of the Spirit."[22]

So if you want to be filled afresh with the Holy Spirit, come with longing and expectancy to the Lord's table and eat and drink His Spirit-filled body and blood. Don't come eat and drink as if it's merely an interlude between the worship and the sermon, as if it's a break from Christ's powerful Spirit-filled presence. No. Come knowing that He has promised to meet you at the table as the glorious, risen and exalted Lord who pours out His Spirit from heaven. Come knowing that as He feeds you with His Spirit-filled body and gives you the Spirit to drink in His blood, you can know the reality of that fresh filling with His Spirit. (And if you haven't been baptized in the Holy Spirit yet, you can receive that first filling at the table, just like they did in Amsterdam.)

The Spirit is always present at the table. We don't always see it, but it's true. Because where Jesus is, the Holy Spirit is too. You cannot divide the Triune God. Sometimes people see the Spirit's presence in powerful ways at the table. Like when people have been baptized in the Spirit at the breaking of bread, or when the Spirit has distributed His gifts around the table, and the supper has been accompanied by prophecy, tongues and interpretation, healings, words of wisdom and knowledge, faith, miracles and the discerning of spirits. (One major Pentecostal leader in Britain had to remind people that the Spirit could actually work by the gifts in other places apart from the Lord's table—that's how much early Pentecostals saw the gifts of the Spirit at the breaking of bread!)

Sometimes the Lord has shown people the presence of His Spirit at the supper in other ways too. A thousand years ago, Symeon ("the New Theologian") was a pastor in Constantinople. When he was ordained, the Holy Spirit fell upon him in a particularly powerful way, described as: "pure and formless like boundless light, coming down and covering his ... head." From then on, every time Symeon celebrated the Lord's Supper, he saw the same light of the Holy Spirit shining on the bread and cup.[23] The Lord reminded Symeon every time he came to the table that the same Holy Spirit who had been powerfully poured out upon him at his ordination was still there, being poured out into him again and again as he ate and drank.

REVIVAL POURED OUT

The Lord has also shown the power of His Spirit at the supper through revivals there too. The powerful presence of the Lord that Howell Harris and Daniel Rowland both experienced in Wales in 1735 sparked off the first Welsh Revival, but that wasn't the only time revival broke out at the Lord's table.

A generation later, Ioan Thomas experienced a powerful outpouring of the Spirit bringing revival to Caebach in south Wales. And it all began one Sunday at Communion.

> The Lord came powerfully down ... especially during the celebration of the Lord's Supper. It was just like the Day of Pentecost. Many cried out when they came under conviction, and others praised the Lord, singing and praying, and speaking to each other ... and many people were added to the church.[24]

When the 1904–1905 Welsh Revival broke out, in many places it was sparked off at Communion services too. At one Communion service the presence of the Lord was so powerfully felt in the supper that one of those distributing the bread and the cup said, "The Holy Presence of God was so terrible that as I went around with the Communion vessels I felt as if they were burning my hands."[25] In Pembrokeshire, the revival began with the outpouring of the Holy Spirit at the Lord's Supper in the village of Nevern. The church there had been founded in the sixth century by Brynach, and it is one of the oldest places of continuous Christian worship in Wales. On that Sunday in 1904 at Holy Communion, the Holy Spirit was poured out in a powerful way that sparked off revival.

In 1859 a revival broke out in what is now Northern Ireland. And again the Lord used Communion to fan the revival into flame. Two years earlier, some believers had started a Sunday school and a prayer meeting in the village of Kells, and before long, people were getting saved every week. The local church was across the bridge in the neighboring village of Connor, and at the Communion there, people began to experience an increased sense of God's presence. One man who got saved in Kells wanted to see other people in his home village of Ahoghill come to Jesus in a living way too. So the people in Kells and Connor began to pray for Ahoghill, and people there started getting saved as well. Then, on March 14, 1859, at the close of the Communion in Ahoghill, there was a powerful outpouring of the Holy Spirit. The congregation moved out from the church into the village square, where, in the pouring rain, the huge crowd stood listening to the Gospel being preached for hours, with many people falling down in the street and crying out to God for His mercy. That was the beginning of the Ulster Awakening of 1859, a revival that had a bigger spiritual impact in Northern Ireland than anything since the days of Saint Patrick. More than a hundred thousand people came to faith in Jesus.

Jesus meets us in His supper. And when Jesus meets us, He can do far beyond what we could ever ask or imagine. So come to the table trusting in Him. Come to the table with faith in His presence. Come to the table with expectation and hunger, knowing that He can meet you in a way so powerful, it goes far beyond just you.

11

Tasting Heaven

EVERY TIME WE COME to the Lord's table, the promise of Christ's return rings out loud and clear. We don't celebrate the breaking of bread in a never-ending way. No. These trips to the table will come to an end. We gather at the supper to proclaim the Lord's death only "till He comes" (1 Corinthians 11:26).

The supper proclaims this blessed hope of Christ's return, and in the meantime, the supper lifts our eyes above, to "where Christ is, sitting at the right hand of God" (Colossians 3:1). The breaking of bread lifts our eyes and our hearts to heaven and fills us more and more with longing for the coming of Christ and His heavenly Kingdom. But the supper doesn't only leave us longing for heaven; it is where heaven meets earth.

WITH ANGELS AND ARCHANGELS

What do you see when you look around your church on the Lord's Day at the breaking of bread? Do you see a bustling crowd? Enthusiastic worshipers? Or lots of empty seats? Sometimes we can get very excited about what we see around us in church. We see crowds and busyness and new faces and we feel good. We feel things are happening. We feel the church is alive. Or maybe we see diminishing numbers of people, or a rapidly aging congregation with no new life, or some missed notes and wonky instruments, and we start to despair. We feel like nothing is happening. We feel like the church is lacking in life.

But don't look around you in either of those ways. Neither is good. Because we are never alone. When we gather around the Lord's table, we gather with the angels and archangels and the whole company of heaven. When you go into the service on Sunday morning, you're surrounded by the heavenly host.

When I pray at the table to give thanks and bless the bread and wine, I always include a few lines that Christians all over the world have prayed for nearly as long as the Church has celebrated the supper, because it expresses what is really going on.

Pastor: Therefore, with angels and archangels
And with the whole company of heaven,
We praise and magnify Your glorious name,
Evermore praising you and saying:
[*Everyone:*] Holy, Holy, Holy, Lord God of Hosts,
Heaven and earth are full of Your glory.
Glory be to You, O Lord most high.

They're just a few lines in the middle of a big prayer of thanksgiving. But as we pray and hear these words, we're brought back to the reality of what's going on. It's not just a bunch of people meeting in an old stone church, or a school assembly hall, or the community center, or the village hall, or the shiny, newly built church building. No. Heaven meets earth at this table, and the angels surround us and join with us as in awe and wonder as we acclaim our holy God. The building (and the congregation in it) might not look all that glorious, but they, along with all heaven and earth, are full of the glory of our saving God. We worship with the angels—and not only angels, but archangels, and the whole company of heaven—as we join them in the song they ever sing in the highest, holiest place in the presence of the Lord (see Isaiah 6:1–3; Revelation 4:8).

In the college chapel at the seminary where I teach, when I pray these words at the table, I look up and get to see something no one else can at that moment. Behind the congregation, I see the large, circular stained-glass window at the far end of the chapel. In the center of the window there's a chalice and a loaf of unleavened bread. The rest of the window is filled with a host of angels gazing at those tokens of Christ's passion. Not many pastors get to see angels while they pray this prayer, but thanks to that window, I do. They might only be stained-glass angels, but they remind me who is really filling the chapel with us as we pray at the Lord's table.

How do I know the angels are there? Well, all our theology has to come from what God has revealed to us in Scripture. We don't believe the angels are there because a prayer tells us; we believe because the Bible tells us they are.

COMING TO MOUNT ZION

Near the end of the book of Hebrews, we find one of the most glorious descriptions of Christian worship, and it looks nothing like the familiar room we sit in every Sunday morning on earth.

> But you have come to Mount Zion and to the city of the living God, the heavenly Jerusalem, to an innumerable company of angels, to the general assembly and church of the firstborn who are registered in heaven, to God the Judge of all, to the spirits of just men made perfect, to Jesus the Mediator of the new covenant, and to the blood of sprinkling that speaks better things than that of Abel.
>
> Hebrews 12:22–24

What does this incredible heavenly host have to do with our breaking-of-bread services on earth? Well, let's have a look at a few details. First, when it says, "You have come to Mount Zion," it's not just *you* individually. It's *you* plural.[1] It's something we do together. Together, we come to Mount Zion. It's something corporate, for the Church.

Second, although this Scripture starts off by telling us we've come to Mount Zion, it builds up from there until it tells us our true destination. We have come to Jesus, the Mediator of the new covenant, and to His sprinkled blood. Where do we as the Church come to Jesus together? When we gather together in His name to worship Him. But, more specifically than that, where do we as the Church come to Jesus' sprinkled blood of the new covenant together? When we come to the Lord's Supper.

Remember Troas. The breaking of bread was *the* reason the early Church gathered together for worship. Yes, they prayed. Yes, they had fellowship with one another. Yes, they listened to the preaching of God's Word. Yes, they moved in the gifts of the Holy Spirit. But the ultimate purpose of their worship services was to break bread (Acts 20:7). The very center of Christian worship—the highest point of our gatherings—has always been, and always should be, meeting with Jesus in the breaking of bread.

And that's what we see in Hebrews. You might think Hebrews doesn't mention the Lord's Supper, but it is a bit like John's gospel. It was written to people who were meeting with the Lord at His table week by week (or maybe even day by day) and *had* been, long before any of the New Testament was written down. While it feels more normal for us to look at the supper in the light of the New Testament (which we always should), for them it was the other way around. They'd had the Lord's Supper from the outset. So they would have read Hebrews in light of that supper they already knew so well. And the writer knew it. He didn't need to explicitly use expressions like *breaking of bread* or *Lord's Supper*, because the Lord's table permeated his letter and would be obvious to his readers. English theologian E. L. Mascall says it well:

> Thus, if from one point of view we are bound to say that there is nothing about the Eucharist [i.e. the Lord's supper] in the Epistle to the Hebrews, from another point of view we might almost say that the Epistle to the Hebrews is about nothing else. For everything that the Epistle describes is given to us in the Eucharist; it would be a pitiful weakening of the theme to make the Eucharist one item in the series.[2]

The early Christians also often preferred to talk about the supper in less-obvious ways, as they considered it too holy a thing for unbelievers to hear about. Early Church documents like *The Apostolic Tradition* show us that when people started coming to church to investigate the Christian faith, they'd be sent home before the breaking of bread. People didn't even get to see the Lord's Supper until after they had become Christians and been baptized. And when newly baptized Christians were taught about the supper, they were reminded that "none but the faithful may know."[3] So it isn't surprising at all to find the supper in the book of Hebrews in a less-than-obvious way.

Third, these verses use an odd expression for the Church. It's called "the general assembly and church of the firstborn" (verse 23). But "general assembly" isn't a frequently used name for the Church in the New Testament. In fact, this is the only verse in the entire New Testament where this word (it's only one word in Greek) is found. Yet that doesn't mean it would be an unfamiliar word to the first people to read the book of Hebrews, because it was a biblical word. It appears four times in the Septuagint (the Greek translation of the Old Testament that was used by the early Church). And each time it comes up there, it's in connection with eating. It's not just a word for the gathering of the Church, but for the joy-filled assembly for a feast of worship.

So these verses in Hebrews 12 are telling us about what happens when the Church corporately gathers in the presence of Jesus and His shed blood of the new covenant to eat and drink in worship. In other words, these verses are telling us about what's going on when we celebrate the Lord's Supper.

And what else do we find? We find "an innumerable company of angels" (verse 22). We could guess that we'd find angels in the presence of the Lord, but we don't have to guess—the Bible tells us explicitly. When we come to Jesus to eat and drink of the new covenant in His blood, we are surrounded by angels and archangels and all the heavenly host. In the breaking of bread, heaven meets earth.

THE COMMUNION OF SAINTS

When heaven meets earth, we don't only join with the angels, we join with the joyful festal assembly of the "church of the firstborn who are registered in heaven" and with "the spirits of just men made perfect" (verse 23). Now, these aren't just two different ways to say the same thing. We are being pointed to two different aspects of the totality of Christ's Church here. The Church "of the firstborn who are registered in heaven" tells us that we're joining with the entire Church around the world and throughout time. We're joining with all those whose names are written in the Lamb's Book of Life (see Revelation 17:8; 21:27). So when we celebrate the Lord's Supper, we're united with all those who are gathering all over the world to break bread. When I come to the Lord's table in my little church in the middle of a graveyard in Wales, I'm joined with my missionary friends as they gather in a village church in the bush in Malawi, and with my university friends in a medieval church in Cambridge, and with my parents in their church on a housing estate in Northern Ireland, and with my sister and her family in an international church in downtown Seoul, and with my brothers and sisters meeting in secret in underground churches in countries where Christ's people face severe persecution, and with the dying believer receiving Communion for the last time in a hospital bed, and with you as you come to the Lord's table in your church, wherever that might be. We're all joined together as we eat and drink of Jesus.

But not only are we all joined together as we meet with Christ at His table in our churches all over the world, we're also joined together with those who have gone before us and those who will come after us. We're joined with the whole Church, not only around the world, but throughout history. We're joined with the disciples who continued steadfastly in the breaking of bread after the Day of Pentecost (see Acts 2:42); with the disciples who came together on the first day of the week in Troas to break bread (see Acts 20:7); with Eutychus, who was raised from death at the supper; and with Tarcisius, who was beaten to death for the supper. We're joined with the martyrs of the early Church, the missionaries who took the Gospel to new parts of the world, and we're joined with all those who are yet to come to faith in Jesus. Because there is only one Church. There isn't a first-century church and a fifth-century church and a twenty-first-century church. There isn't a medieval church and a Reformation church and a modern church. Christ only has one body. And as we all partake of Him as our Bread of Life, He bakes us all together into "one bread and one body" (1 Corinthians 10:17), throughout the world and throughout the ages. Time and geography aren't insurmountable barriers to Jesus.

This passage in Hebrews 12 also tells us that when we gather for this heavenly meal at the Lord's table, we come "to the spirits of just men made perfect." Those who have died in Christ are there, because they are united to Christ. They haven't disappeared. They haven't been forgotten about. They rest in Jesus and live in His presence as they await the resurrection day, when their bodies will be raised from their graves and transformed to be like His glorious body (see Philippians 3:21). And at the Lord's table, where heaven meets earth, those who live now in the presence of the Lord in heaven join with us in worship around the table and throne of God. So at the table, in communion with our Savior Head, we have fellowship with the members of His body who have been made perfect in His presence. As a pastor from the Bronx put it, at the table "we join hands not only with the great saints in heaven, but also with our loved ones who have passed within the veil, our faithful departed."[4]

Now, we should be careful here. The supper is not a séance. We don't come to the Lord's table to speak to the dead. We don't want to be like Saul and fall into witchcraft to find a word from beyond the grave (see 1 Samuel 28:3–25). The supper is not a means to start communicating with the dead. The supper is far better than that. For in it we have not communication, but communion. Communion with those who have died in Christ is only possible in communion with Christ. For Christ has united Himself to His people, and they dwell in Him. As we meet with Christ in the supper, through communion with Him we have communion with those we have lost who live in Him. (In our bereavements and mourning, we can draw near to Jesus in the supper and find true comfort and joy for our broken hearts.)

TO GOD AND TO JESUS

The most glorious presence at the supper isn't the presence of the angels or the saints; it is the presence of God and of the Lamb. The Lord's Supper is not a reminder of an absent Lord, but a feast in the presence of God, the Judge of all, where we are fed with the presence of Jesus, the Mediator of the new covenant. The saints and angels, the Church past, present and future, are all only present because the Lord Himself is present.

Think of a royal wedding. Kings, queens, princes, princesses, prime ministers, presidents, lords, ladies, celebrities, politicians, ambassadors and all sorts of other glittering and glorious people come together in Westminster Abbey or an equally glorious location. And if you were invited, you might be overwhelmed at the presence of so many celebrated figures in one room. Yet they're not the point; they're only there because the bride and groom are there. And when the royal bride enters the church, no one's looking at the king of Sweden or the prince of Monaco or the prime minister of Japan or the winner of Wimbledon. At other times, they might get all the attention in whatever room they're in. But not in this room. Not at this moment. Something much more glorious is going on. And all eyes are fixed on the bride and groom.

The same is true of the Lord's Supper. Yes, the angels and archangels, the cherubim and seraphim gather with us. Yes, the saints throughout the ages are there. But there is a much more glorious presence on which all eyes are fixed. The presence of the Lord Himself, the King of Glory. The Judge of all is there. Yet He is there inviting us to come and taste His mercy as we taste of His Son.

God Himself sits enthroned at the Lord's table. He is the Master of this feast. He bids us come and welcomes us in. He feeds us with the body and blood of His Son. This is the foretaste of the wedding feast to come.

THE BLOOD OF SPRINKLING

At the table, we meet with Jesus as the Mediator of the new covenant where He gives us His blood to drink. But Hebrews tells us we've come to "the blood of sprinkling" (Hebrews 12:24). So what is the sprinkling?

In the Levitical sacrifices of the Old Testament, all sorts of things were done with blood. Blood was poured, daubed and dashed. But in only one case was blood truly sprinkled. The blood of sprinkling was the blood of public sin offering, for in that sacrifice the blood was sprinkled either "before the LORD, in front of the veil" of the Holy of Holies (Leviticus 4:17), or, once a year on the Day of Atonement, inside the Holy of Holies on the Mercy Seat over the Ark of the Covenant (Leviticus 16:14–15). Then the rest of the blood was shed (or poured out) at the base of the altar (Leviticus 4:18).[5]

Now, we've already seen how Jesus is our true sin offering, whom we eat and drink in the supper. So the blood He gives us to drink in the breaking of bread is sin-offering blood. Under the Old Covenant the blood shed for the remission of sins was sprinkled. But the blood of the New Covenant is far greater and comes much closer to us. In the New Covenant the blood of sprinkling is drunk. Now our hearts are sprinkled by the atoning blood of the Lamb of God, who takes away the sins of the world. The sprinkling of the New Covenant takes place internally, as we drink the cup of blessing, which is a participation in the blood of Christ.

There was one other time when blood was sprinkled in a different way in a unique sacrifice that took place before the Levitical system was set in place. Back in Exodus 24, before Moses and elders of Israel went up the mountain and saw the Lord above the sapphire pavement and ate and drank in His presence, they "offered burnt offerings and sacrificed peace offerings of oxen to the LORD" (Exodus 24:5). Then Moses read the covenant to the people, and they affirmed it. And after that, "Moses took the blood, sprinkled it on the people, and said, 'This is the blood of the covenant which the LORD has made with you according to all these words'" (Exodus 24:8).

This unique sprinkling of blood was the institution of the Old Covenant. The people who had been brought into covenant relationship with the Lord through His mighty act of deliverance in the Passover and the Exodus were sprinkled with the blood of the covenant. And then, when Jesus instituted the New Covenant, the same thing happened. That same proclamation was made: This is the blood of the covenant. But now, instead of being physically sprinkled with the blood, in the New Covenant we drink the blood, and it's our hearts that are sprinkled within us. In the Old Covenant, the blood never came nearer than that sprinkling. But in the New Covenant, the blood of the true Lamb of God gets as close to us as it's possible to get, as it's poured into our mouths. And "having our hearts sprinkled" within by that drinking of Christ's blood, we can boldly draw near into the true Holy of Holies of God's presence "by the blood of Jesus, by a new and living way which He consecrated for us, through the veil, that is, His flesh" (Hebrews 10:19–20).

In the Lord's Supper, we draw near into the Holy of Holies. Heaven meets earth, and we gather in worship with the angels and archangels and the whole company of heaven. We're joined with the whole Church around the world and throughout the ages. But above all, we come into the presence of God Himself, the Judge of all, as we feed upon the presence of Jesus, our sin offering, who sprinkles our hearts with His precious, cleansing blood. That's what's really going on each Sunday morning when we gather 'round the Lord's table.

TASTING OF THE POWERS OF THE AGE TO COME

Earlier in the book of Hebrews, we find a description of some of the privileges of those who belong to Jesus. Christ's people are those who have been "enlightened, and have tasted the heavenly gift, and have become partakers of the Holy Spirit, and have tasted the good word of God and the powers of the age to come" (Hebrews 6:4–5). Although our hearts were darkened in sin, Christ has shone into our darkness and opened our eyes to His glorious light (John 8:12; 12:46; Acts 26:18; Romans 1:21; Ephesians 4:18). And now, enlightened by the Light of the World, He makes us partakers of the Holy Spirit and tasters of the heavenly gift, the good word of God and the powers of the age to come.

Now, remember what we've seen about Hebrews. Although this letter never mentions the supper by name, it constantly presupposes the centrality of the supper in the life of its readers. Just before these verses is one of the places where people are most surprised not to find an explicit mention of the supper in this letter. There we read about "the foundation of repentance from dead works and of faith toward God, of the doctrine of baptisms, of laying on of hands, of resurrection of the dead, and of eternal judgment" (Hebrews 6:1–2). We get a list of basic foundations, including baptism, but without the supper. But then in verse 4, the writer immediately turns our attention to people who taste and partake.

Taste and *partake* are both words that go with what we eat and drink in the Lord's Supper. Paul uses a form of the same word for partaking when he writes that "we, though many, are one bread and one body; for we all partake of that one bread" (1 Corinthians 10:17) and that "you cannot partake of the Lord's table and of the table of demons" (1 Corinthians 10:21). Christians partake of the Holy Spirit in several different ways. He is the One who has convicted us of our sins, opened our eyes to our need of Christ for salvation, lifted us out of our death in sin and united us to Christ for salvation and new life. Jesus also promises to baptize believers in the Holy Spirit, but as we've seen earlier, one of the ways we partake of the Spirit is in partaking of the Spirit-filled body and blood of Jesus in the supper, where we are all given one Spirit to drink (see 1 Corinthians 12:13). Hebrews doesn't specify one particular way of receiving the Spirit here, but the word *partake* at least reminds us that one of those ways is in the supper.

The word *taste* reminds us even more of eating and drinking of Christ in the supper. Hebrews says we taste three things: the heavenly gift, the good word of God and the powers of the age to come (see Hebrews 6:4–5). Now, in Christ's salvation, we receive a richness of heavenly gifts and experience so much of the power of the age to come. And throughout this life of salvation, we taste the sweetness of God's Word in many ways as well. We taste the goodness of God's Word as we read and meditate on the Scriptures, as we hear the Word read and preached in church and even as we sing Scripture songs and psalms. Not only do we taste the goodness of the written Word, but we also taste the sweetness of the Incarnate Word, the Lord Jesus, as we eat the bread and drink the wine of the supper. *Taste* is an especially appropriate word to direct our attention to that.

And given that it's in the context of tasting the heavenly gift, it looks like our attention is being intentionally drawn that way. For what is the heavenly gift? Well, ultimately, of course, Jesus Himself is our heavenly gift. Earlier, Hebrews spoke of sacrifices as gifts (see Hebrews 5:1), and it's only as the One who is our perfect sacrifice that we taste Jesus. It's in the supper that we actually taste that once-for-all sacrifice as we receive Christ's body and blood, and in them taste the goodness of the Lord (see Psalm 34:8; 1 Peter 2:3).[6]

We taste Christ, who is our salvation, in the supper, and both the gift and the taste are heavenly. With our mouths, we taste bread and wine, but through the eyes of faith we see that this is not just an earthly meal. He reaches down from heaven by His body and blood, conveyed to us in bread and wine, to lift us up to heaven, where we are seated together with Him (see Ephesians 2:6). The bread we break and the cup of blessing we bless are the very portals of heaven, bringing Christ to us and us to Christ. When heaven meets earth as we taste this heavenly gift, we taste of the powers of the age to come. Tasting of heaven doesn't just mean that it's a nice taste or a nice feeling. Heaven is the place of the presence of the Lord. Heaven is where Jesus is at the right hand of the Father, the hand He stretches out to perform His mighty works. God's "right hand has stretched out the heavens" (Isaiah 48:13) and "has dashed the enemy in pieces" (Exodus 15:6). By His right hand, the Lord shows His "marvelous lovingkindness" (Psalm 17:7) and upholds His people (Psalm 18:35; 63:8; 73:23; 139:10). The Lord's right hand is where we find both "saving strength" (Psalm 20:6) and "pleasures forevermore" (Psalm 16:11). "His right hand and His holy arm have gained Him the victory" (Psalm 98:1). The right hand of the Lord is "full of righteousness" (Psalm 48:10), and by His right hand, the Lord does valiantly (see Psalm 118:15–16) and saves (see Psalms 60:5; 108:6; 138:7).

So, when heaven meets earth in the supper, we encounter the right hand of God stretched out in mighty power, in glorious grace, in loving-kindness, in saving strength and in merciful compassion. When heaven meets earth, heaven's power is at hand, because the Lord stretches out His hand.

The power of heaven is the power of the age to come. It doesn't belong to this age or this world. It belongs to the One who dwells beyond this age and fills eternity. It belongs to the One who spoke this world into being, who upholds every star and every planet, every atom and everything unseen by His infinite power. This is the heavenly power we taste at the table, because this is Christ's power, and at the table we partake of Him.

All things are possible for the Lord we meet in the supper. But we come to meet Him there in His heavenly presence not because we want to merely taste His gifts. We come because we want to taste Him, the High King of Heaven.

In the breaking of bread, we "proclaim the Lord's death till He comes" (1 Corinthians 11:26), and we long for His return. Until that day when Christ returns from heaven, His Supper brings heaven to earth and earth to heaven as we worship around the Lord's table-throne with angels and archangels and the whole company of heaven, and taste in Him of the powers of the age to come. But that foretaste of heaven is only a glimpse of the glorious future heavenly feast.

Christ will come, and we will feast with Him in glory. We can't even begin to imagine the wonder of that communion. But until that day, we gather as His people around His table to proclaim the Lord's death and meet with our Savior as He feeds us with His body and blood. He has promised His presence. And when He is there, every spiritual blessing is to be found in Him. Yet, we seek the Giver, not merely the gifts. There is nothing more glorious than the presence of Jesus, for there is no one more glorious than Christ our Lord, who lives and reigns with the Father and the Spirit—one God, now and forever.

So come with joy. Come with expectancy, longing and anticipation. Come filled with faith to the table of the Lord. And there behold the Lamb of God, who takes away the sin of the world. Come to the supper and taste and see that the Lord is good.

Lord, open our eyes in the breaking of bread and let our hearts burn within us in Your presence! Amen.

NOTES

Chapter 2 The Holy One in Our Midst

1. Damasus of Rome, Latin Inscription in the Catacombs, translation from https://www.christianiconography.info/metropolitan/medieval 5thAvenue/tarcisiusFalguiere.html#poem.

2. Martin Luther, *The Babylonian Captivity of the Church*, in *Three Treatises* (Philadelphia: Fortress Press, 1970), 135.

3. Luther, *The Babylonian Captivity*, 142.

4. Luther, *The Babylonian Captivity*, 147.

5. Luther, *The Babylonian Captivity*, 146.

6. Luther, *The Babylonian Captivity*, 149.

7. Luther, *The Babylonian Captivity*, 152.

8. This is Luther's harmony of the four biblical accounts of the Words of Institution, taken from his *Small Catechism*. https://thesmallcatechism .org/home/the-sacrament-of-the-altar/.

9. We have accounts of the incident from both John Hachenburg, a pastor who was visiting Wittenberg at the time, and Johan Oldecop, a student at Wittenberg who had Luther for his pastor. For a translation of Hachenburg's account, see Edward Peters, "The Origin and Meaning of the Axiom, 'Nothing Has the Character of a Sacrament Outside of the Use,'" Doctor of Theology Dissertation (Concordia Seminary, St Louis, 1968), 191.

10. Thomas Lawson, *The Life of John Calvin* (London: Wileman, 1884), 189.

11. Theodore Beza, *The Life of John Calvin*, in *Tracts Relating to the Reformation by John Calvin with his Life by Theodore Beza*, translated by Henry Beveridge (Edinburgh: Calvin Translation Society, 1844), volume 1, page xiii.

12. Charles Spurgeon, "Mysterious Visits," in *Till He Come: A Collection of Communion Addresses* (Fearn, Ross-shire: Christian Focus, 2010), 12.

13. Charles Spurgeon, "The Well-Beloved," in *Till He Come*, 70.

14. Martin Luther, "Small Catechism," The Evangelical Lutheran Church of England, 2016, https://thesmallcatechism.org/home/the -sacrament-of-the-altar/.

15. Martin Luther, "Confession Concerning Christ's Supper," in *Luther's Works*, volume 37 (Philadelphia: Fortress Press, 1961), 317.

16. His Christian name can also be spelled Huldrych.

17. Ulrich Zwingli, "Exposition of the Faith," *On Providence and Other Essays* (Durham: Labyrinth Press, 1983), 248.

18. Ulrich Zwingli, "Letter to the German Princes," cited in Charles Porterfield Krauth, *The Conservative Reformation and Its Theology* (Philadelphia: Fortress, 1963), 493.

19. John Calvin, "Confession of Faith Concerning the Eucharist," in *Calvin: Theological Treatises* (Philadelphia: Westminster Press, 1954), 168.

20. Anglican Church in North America Committee for Catechesis, *To Be a Christian: An Anglican Catechism* (Wheaton: Crossway, 2020), Q.133.

21. *The Faith Once Delivered: A Wesleyan Witness* (Alexandria, VA: John Wesley Institute, 2022), par. 173.

22. *An Apostolic Confession of the Beauty of the Unity and Diversity of the Body of Christ* (Luton: Apostolic Church UK, 2022), section 7.

23. The Anabaptists took a very similar view to Zwingli on the supper. E.g., Menno Simons, *Foundation of Christian Doctrine*, in *The Complete Writings of Menno Simons*, edited by J. C. Wenger, translated by Leonard Verduin (Scottdale, PA: Herald Press, 1984), 153. Zwingli's view did not make it into any major post-Reformation confession of faith, as the Reformed churches came to accept Calvin's teaching instead. Thus, confessional Protestants followed along the lines of either Calvin or Luther.

24. Pastor Éric Maréchal, Ath Apostolic Church, Sunday May 8, 2022. My translation from French.

25. George Canty, *In My Father's House: Pentecostal Explorations of the Major Christian Truths* (London: Marshall, Morgan & Scott, 1969), 58.

26. Donald Gee, "A Visit to Elim," *Elim Evangel*, May 1923, 81.

27. William J. Seymour, "The Ordinances Taught by Our Lord," *The Apostolic Faith* 1.10, Sept. 1907, 2. D. P. Williams wrote almost identical words in the UK: "We drink His blood; we eat His flesh." D. P. Williams, *Riches of Grace* 11.1 (Sept. 1935), 205.

28. Minutes of the General Council of the Apostolic Church (1928), 144.

29. B. S. Gibson, "Australia," *Confidence* 10.1 (Jan.–Feb. 1917), 9.

30. David Fisher, "Pentecostal Items," *Confidence* 8.12 (Dec. 1915), 237.

Chapter 3 Proclaiming the Cross

1. The Bible doesn't give many detailed instructions for the pouring out of the drink offerings, but we do have historical evidence that in Jesus' day, wine was poured out as a drink offering at the base of the altar during the Feast of Tabernacles. For a widely available account, see Alfred Edersheim, *The Temple: Its Ministry and Sacrifices as They Were at the Time of Jesus Christ* (London: The Religious Tract Society, 1874), 241–242.

2. From Horatius Bonar's hymn for the Lord's Supper, "Here, O My Lord, I See Thee Face to Face." Public Domain.

3. Another verse from Bonar's "Here, O My Lord, I See Thee Face to Face."

Chapter 4 Holy Ground

1. This has been a common part of the Communion service across the Christian church since at least the fourth century, and it quite possibly dates back to the first century.

2. Andrew Murray, *The Lord's Table* (London: Oliphants, 1962), 24.

3. Martin Luther, "Small Catechism," The Evangelical Lutheran Church of England, 2016, https://thesmallcatechism.org/home/the-sacrament-of-the-altar/.

4. Martin Luther, *Large Catechism* V.70, 72–73 (translation from https://bookofconcord.org/large-catechism/sacrament-of-the-altar/).

5. William Bradshaw, "A Preparation to the Receiving of Christ's Body and Blood: A Brief Form of Examination," in William Bradshaw and Arthur Hildersham, *Preparing for the Lord's Supper* (Grand Rapids: Soli Deo Gloria, 2019), 96.

6. Thomas Watson, *The Doctrine of Repentance* (Edinburgh: Banner of Truth, 1987), 28.

7. Watson, *Doctrine of Repentance*, 29.

8. Mark Jones, *Knowing Sin: Seeing a Neglected Doctrine Through the Eyes of the Puritans* (Chicago: Moody, 2022), 67.

9. Johann Gerhard, *Succinct and Select Theological Aphorisms* (Malone, TX: Repristination Press, 2018), 106.

10. Prayer of Humble Access, modernized version from the Church of Ireland's 2004 *Book of Common Prayer* (Norwich: Canterbury Press, 2018), 207.

Chapter 5 One Bread, One Body

1. Irenaeus of Lyons, *Against Heresies*, Book 5, preface. This translation is from Robert M. Grant, *Irenaeus of Lyons*, The Early Church Fathers (London: Routledge, 1997), 164.

2. Catesby Paget, "A Mind at Perfect Peace with God." Public Domain.

3. Raniero Cantalamessa, *The Eucharist, Our Sanctification* (Collegeville, MN: Liturgical Press, 1995), 38.

4. Matthew the Poor, *Words for Our Time* (Chesterton, IN: Ancient Faith Publishing, 2012), 192.

5. W. F. P. Burton, *What Mean Ye by These Stones?: Bible Talks on the Lord's Table* (London: Victory Press, 1947), 9.

6. Burton, *What Mean Ye by These Stones?*, 92.

7. Burton, *What Mean Ye by These Stones?*, 96.

Chapter 6 Wonder-Working Power

1. John Calvin used this image in the *Catechism of the Church of Geneva*.

2. *Didache*, chapter 8. The *Didache* was written in the first century and was probably completed before the final books of the New Testament.

3. John Wesley, *The Duty of Constant Communion* (Sermon 101).

4. This prayer was prayed at the Lord's table in the Sakumono Assembly of the Apostolic Church in Ghana in 2020 by Pastor Johnson Obong.

5. For the difference between union and communion, see chapter 8.

6. D. A. Carson shows that the jars would have contained between 100 and 150 gallons (or 500 and 750 liters). That's the equivalent of somewhere between 670 and 1000 wine bottles. D. A. Carson, *The Gospel According to John*, Pillar New Testament Commentary (Nottingham: Apollos, 1991), 173.

Chapter 7 Jesus, Our Manna

1. Jonathan Fisk, *Without Flesh: Why the Church Is Dying Even Though Jesus Is Still Alive* (St. Louis: Concordia, 2020), 70.

2. Adolph Saphir, "The Lord's Supper and the Passover," in Gavin Carlyle, *Mighty in the Scriptures: A Memoir of Adolph Saphir* (New York: Fleming Revell, 1893), 358

3. Cyril of Alexandria, *Commentary on John*, Volume 1 (Downers Grove: IVP, 2013), 246.

4. Although, if you want to see me set out an argument for my view, see another book of mine, *Apostolic Theology: A Trinitarian, Evangelical, Pentecostal Introduction to Christian Doctrine* (Luton: Apostolic Church UK, 2016), 599–623.

5. Johann Gerhard, *Sacred Meditations* (Saginaw, MI: Magdeburg Press, 2008), 81–82.

6. D. P. Williams, *Riches of Grace*, 11.1 (September 1935), 205.

7. Apostolic Church General Council Minutes for 1928, 144.

8. D. P. Williams, *Shewbread*, 9. Manuscript from the archives of the Apostolic Church, UK.

Chapter 8 I Stand Amazed in the Presence

1. Charles Spurgeon, "The Well-Beloved's Vineyard," *Till He Come: A Collection of Communion Addresses* (Fearn, Ross-shire: Christian Focus, 1970), 106.

2. Charles Spurgeon, "The Well-Beloved," *Till He Come*, 70.

3. C. S. Lewis, *The Weight of Glory* (London: William Collins, 2013), 26.

4. John Owen, *Communion with God* (Edinburgh: Banner of Truth, 1991), 2. Owen was a wonderful theologian, but very difficult to read, especially as he wrote in seventeenth-century English. So I quote him from the excellent "abridged and made easy to read" edition edited by R. J. K. Law in the Puritan Paperbacks series. If you'd like to read Owen for your own spiritual benefit, that is the best version to get.

5. Owen, *Communion with God*, 59.

6. Willison, *Sacramental Catechism* (Pittsburgh: Loomis, 1830), 59–60.

7. Wilhelmus à Brakel, *The Christian's Reasonable Service*, vol. 2 (Grand Rapids: Reformation Heritage Books, 2015), 573–574.

8. Donald Gee, "A Visit to Elim," *Elim Evangel* (May 1923), 81.

9. À Brakel, *The Christian's Reasonable Service*, 2:464.

10. À Brakel, *The Christian's Reasonable Service*, 2:456.

11. À Brakel, *The Christian's Reasonable Service*, 2:93.

12. Murray, *The Lord's Table*, 91.

13. Adolph Saphir, *The Hidden Life: Thoughts on Communion with God* (Glasgow: Pickering & Inglis, 1917), 170.

14. D. P. Williams, "Mae rhyw ddyheadau cryfion," *Molwch Dduw* (Penygroes: Apostolic Church, 1952), 315. This is my literal translation from the original Welsh.

15. D. Caleb Morgan, "Apart with God," *Riches of Grace*, 2.1 (July 1921), 29.

16. "Banqueting house" makes sense in English, but the Hebrew is literally "a house of wine."

17. Symeon the New Theologian, "One Hundred and Fifty-Three Practical and Theological Texts," 153, in *The Philokalia*, volume 4 (New York: Farrar, Straus & Giroux, 1995), 62–63.

18. Isaac Ambrose, "Communion with Angels," in *Works of Isaac Ambrose* (London: Caxton Press, 1800), 527–528.

19. These extracts from Isaac Ambrose's diary are reproduced in Tom Schwanda, *Soul Recreation: The Contemplative-Mystical Piety of Puritanism* (Eugene, OR: Pickwick, 2012), 110.

20. The book was Lewis Bayly's *The Practice of Piety*. Bayly was a Puritan who became Bishop of Bangor in Wales.

21. The Diary of Howell Harris as translated and cited in Richard Bennett, *Howell Harris and the Dawn of Revival* (Bridgend: Evangelical Press of Wales, 1962), 26.

22. Daniel Rowland, Letter to George Whitefield, February 2, 1743, printed in Eifion Evans, *Daniel Rowland and the Great Evangelical Awakening in Wales* (Edinburgh: Banner of Truth, 1985), 74.

23. Rowland, *Great Evangelical Awakening*, 74.

24. Kathleen Stuart, in *Autobiographical Accounts of Persons Under Spiritual Concern at Cambuslang During the Revival of 1741–1743* (Oswestry: Quinta Press, 2008), 1:164–165, http://quintapress.webmate.me /PDF_Books/Cambuslang_Testimonies_Vol_1.pdf.

25. Rebecca Dykes, in *Autobiographical Accounts*, 1:189.

26. James Tenant, in *Autobiographical Accounts*, 1:282.

27. R. Barclay, in *Autobiographical Accounts*, 1:232.

28. Catherine Cameron, in *Autobiographical Accounts*, 1:219.

29. Catherine Cameron, in *Autobiographical Accounts*, 1:214.

30. Catherine Cameron, in *Autobiographical Accounts*, 1:214.

31. The reason not everyone was admitted to the Lord's table was because people had to be examined by the elders first to check that they were believers, that they understood what the supper was about and that they weren't under church discipline. A lot of people traveled from all over Scotland and the north of England for these services in Cambuslang, so they weren't part of a local church in the area to be able to have the

elders admit them to the table. Bear in mind, only eighteen thousand people lived in Glasgow at the time.

32. Catherine Cameron, in *Autobiographical Accounts*, 1:215.

33. Ann Montgomery, *Autobiographical Accounts*, 2:148.

34. David Charles, Letter from Trefeca College, November 8, 1859, reproduced in D. Geraint Jones, *Favoured With Frequent Revivals: Revivals in Wales 1762–1862* (Cardiff: Heath Christian Trust, 2001), 106–113.

35. D. Caleb Morgan, "The Annual Convention, Penygroes, August 1922," *Riches of Grace* 2.3 (November 1922), 24.

36. E. C. W. Boulton, "Great Gatherings at the Hull Convention," *Elim Evangel* (May 1923), 78.

37. Alexander Boddy, "The German Conference: December 1908," *Confidence* (January 1909), 4; Alexander Boddy, *Special Supplement to Confidence No. 9* (December 1908), 4.

38. A. J. Tomlinson, "Fourth of July at Tabernacle," *The Evening Light and Church of God Evangel* 1.10 (July 15, 1910), 1.

39. Burton, *What Mean Ye*, 26.

40. Burton, *What Mean Ye*, 43.

41. Burton, *What Mean Ye*, 53.

42. The original book was called *A Spiritual Supper*, but a few years later it became half of a bigger book called *Efficacy of the Lord's Supper to the Comfort and Sanctification of God's Children*. It is published today along with a book by another Dutch pastor: Guilelmus Saldenus & Wilhelmus à Brakel, *In Remembrance of Him: Profiting from the Lord's Supper* (Grand Rapids: Reformation Heritage, 2012).

43. Saldenus, "Efficacy of the Lord's Supper," in Saldenus & à Brakel, *In Remembrance of Him*, 21.

44. Saldenus, "Efficacy of the Lord's Supper," 22.

45. Saldenus, "Efficacy of the Lord's Supper," 23.

46. Saldenus, "Efficacy of the Lord's Supper," 22.

47. Saldenus, "Efficacy of the Lord's Supper," 22.

48. Saldenus, "Efficacy of the Lord's Supper," 22.

Chapter 9 Every Spiritual Blessing

1. This is the response to "Holy things for holy people" that was used in the liturgy of the Catholic Apostolic Church, a nineteenth-century forerunner to Pentecostalism.

2. J. B. Clyne and Hugh Mitchell, "Taste the Bread of Sweet Communion," *Gospel Quintet Choruses* (Bradford, UK: The Apostolic Church), 10:480. Used with permission.

3. John Kleinig, *Leviticus* (St Louis: Concordia, 2003), 5–6.

4. Kleinig, *Leviticus*, 10–11.

5. Cyril of Alexandria, *Commentary on John*, volume 1 (Downers Grove: IVP, 2015), 239.

6. John Owen, *The Mortification of Sin* (Edinburgh: Banner of Truth, 2004), 5. This is a wonderful book on this vital aspect of the Christian life. As usual when it comes to John Owen, I recommend the "abridged and made easy to read" version (this time prepared by Richard Rushing) in the Puritan Paperbacks series.

7. Stephen Charnock, "Discourses on the Lord's Supper," *The Works of Stephen Charnock*, volume 4 (Edinburgh: Banner of Truth, 1985), 408–409. I have slightly modernized Charnock's verb endings.

8. John Owen, *The Mortification of Sin*, 18.

9. John Owen, *The Mortification of Sin*, 128.

10. John Owen, *The Mortification of Sin*, 116.

11. Willison, *Sacramental Meditations and Advices* (Edinburgh: Thomas Lumisden, 1747), 80. Lightly modernized.

12. Isaac Ambrose, *Media: The Middle Things or the Means for Continuance and Increase of a Godly Life, in Prima, Media, et Ultima*, 7th edition (Glasgow: James Knox, 1777), 315.

13. Ambrose, *Media*, 315.

14. Ambrose, *Media*, 316.

15. Leo the Great, Sermon 12 on the Passion, 7.

16. Johann Gerhard, *A Comprehensive Explanation of Holy Baptism and the Lord's Supper (1610)*, translated by Elmer Hohle (Malone, TX: Repristination Press, 2014), 368.

17. Martin Chemnitz, "The Lord's Supper," translated by J. A. O. Preus, in *Chemnitz's Works Volume 5* (St. Louis, MO: Concordia, 2007), 143.

Chapter 10 The Power of His Presence

1. Edwin Williams, "The Lord's Supper," *Riches of Grace* 7.5 (May 1932): 214. Every biblical account of the institution of the supper makes clear that Jesus gave the disciples a single cup to share. And there are important theological reasons for this. In recent years, various epidemics have led to a number of scientific studies into the possibility of transmission of disease via the chalice (by scientists who do not take account of Christ's presence).

All have been in general agreement that "no episode of disease attributable to the shared communion cup has ever been reported. Currently available data do not provide any support for suggesting that the practice of sharing a common communion cup should be abandoned because it might spread infection." O. Noel Gill, "The Hazard of Infection from the Shared Communion Cup," *Journal of Infection* 16.1 (January 1988): 3. "The risk is so small that it is undetectable. The CDC has not been called on to investigate any episodes or outbreaks of infectious diseases that have been allegedly linked to the use of a common communion cup." Lilia P. Manangan, Lynne M. Sehulster, Linda Chiarello, Dawn N. Simonds, & William R. Jarvis, "Risk of Infectious Disease Transmission from a Common Communion Cup," *American Journal of Infection Control* 26.5 (October 1998), 538–539. In fact, individual cups tend to have more germs, as the rims are touched by people's fingers (which have more germs than lips). The same is true of dipping the bread into the chalice (intinction) due to contamination by fingers.

2. W. J. Jones, "A Modern Miracle: Tuberculosis Healed in 1915," *Redemption Tidings*, August 1925, 9.

3. N. Kennedy, "Personality Spotlight," *Elim Evangel* 38.41 (October 1957), 645.

4. O. C. Wilkins, *Pentecostal Holiness Advocate*, 4.5 (June 3, 1920), 5.

5. Jeremy Taylor, *The Rule and Exercises of Holy Dying* (Cambridge: Dutton, 1876), 306.

6. Matthew Henry, *The Communicant's Companion* (Boston: Crocker & Brewster, 1828), 186.

7. Taylor, *Holy Dying*, 309.

8. *Heidelberg Catechism*, Q.1, translation taken from https://students.wts.edu/resources/creeds/heidelberg.html.

9. The earliest Christians called the supper the Medicine of Immortality for this reason. See Ignatius of Antioch, *Letter to the Ephesians*, 20.

10. Johann Gerhard, *Sacred Meditations*, 80.

11. Cyril of Alexandria, "Explanation of the Twelve Chapters," 25, in John McGuckin, *Saint Cyril of Alexandria and the Christological Controversy* (Crestwood, NY: St. Vladimir's Seminary Press, 2004), 290–291.

12. Ephrem the Syrian, Hymn Ten, *The Hymns on Faith*, translated by Jeffrey T. Wickes (Washington, DC: CUA, 2015), 10:8, 10:17 (122, 124).

13. Symeon the New Theologian, *The Mystical Life: The Ethical Discourses*, Volume 1: The Church and the Last Things (Crestwood, NY: St. Vladimir's Seminary Press, 1995), 180.

14. Symeon, *The Mystical Life*, 181.

15. Gerrit Polman, "Pastor Polman of Amsterdam," *Confidence* (August 1911), 177.

16. H. J. Mason, "Holy Ghost Showers at Coventry," *Redemption Tidings* 11.16 (August 15, 1935), 11.

17. Bernard Tovell, "Enfield," *Redemption Tidings* 9.6 (June 1933), 8.

18. "Welcome News of Widespread Revival," *Elim Evangel* 18.1 (January 1, 1937), 13.

19. "Girl of 15 Baptized in Holy Spirit During Communion Service," *Elim Evangel* 36.32 (August 20, 1955), 374.

20. "Unparalleled Blessing in East Ham," *Elim Evangel* 7.10 (May 15, 1926), 110.

21. Aimee Semple McPherson, "The Baptism in the Holy Ghost: Personal Testimony of Mrs Aimee Semple McPherson," *Elim Evangel* (June 1924), 121.

22. Simon Chan, *Pentecostal Theology and the Christian Spiritual Tradition* (Sheffield: Sheffield Academic Press, 2000), 95–96.

23. Niketas Stethatos, *The Life of Saint Symeon the New Theologian*, translated by Richard P. H. Greenfield (Cambridge, MA: Harvard University Press, 2013), 67. Niketas was a disciple of Symeon and knew him well.

24. Ioan Thomas, *Rhad Ras* (Cardiff: Gwasg Prifysgol Cymru, 1949), 102–103. Translation from David Edward Pryce, "From Poverty to Power: Ioan Thomas, Revivalist," *Welldigger* (May 14, 2017).

25. Brynmor Pierce Jones, *The King's Champions: Revival and Reaction*, 1905–1935 (Glascoed, 1986), 53.

Chapter 11 Tasting Heaven

1. Like in French or Spanish or Welsh (or a whole host of other languages), Greek distinguishes between *you* singular and *you* plural. We can't see it easily in modern English because we've lost the grammatical distinction. But in the King James Version, you'll see this passage uses *ye* (the plural), not *thou* (the singular).

2. E. L. Mascall, *Corpus Christi* (London: Longmans, 1953), 109.

3. Hippolytus, *The Apostolic Tradition*, 21.40.

4. Berthold von Schenk, *The Presence: An Approach to Holy Communion* (Delhi, NY: American Lutheran Publicity Bureau, 2010), 118.

5. In English translations, the word *sprinkle* is sometimes used for what's done with the blood in some of the other sacrifices. But this is actually

a different Hebrew word that involves a lot more blood being splashed up against the sides of the altar. What's done with the blood of the sin offering is a true sprinkling.

6. British evangelical biblical scholar F. F. Bruce sees the supper, along with "the whole sum of spiritual blessings which are sacramentally sealed and signified in the [supper]," as the heavenly gift we taste. F. F. Bruce, *The Epistle to the Hebrews* (Grand Rapids: Eerdmans, 1990), 146.

Jonathan Black, PhD, is an ordained pastor and teacher in the Apostolic Church and lecturer in theology at Regents Theological College, West Malvern, UK, where he is also co-director of the Institute for Pentecostal Theology. Originally from Northern Ireland, he studied theology at University of Cambridge (MA), Continental Theological Seminary/University of Wales (MTh) and University of Chester (PhD). He served on leadership at a church in Brussels, where he also taught at a theological college, and pastored a church in Leeds. Find out more at www.apostolictheology.org.